WISEBLOOD ESSAYS IN CONTEMPORARY CULTURE NO. 17

A THEOLOGY OF FICTION

Cassandra Nelson

WISEBLOOD BOOKS
2025

WISEBLOOD BOOKS
Joshua Hren, Editor-in-Chief
Post Office Box 870
Menomonee Falls, WI 53052
www.wisebloodbooks.com

Printed in the United States of America

ISBN: 978-1-963319-86-6

CONTENTS

for Christopher and Evelyn

PREFACE

This book began as an essay titled "A Theology of Fiction" that appeared in the April 2022 issue of *First Things*. In it, I aimed to bring the lively and incisive literary criticism of Sister Mariella Gable to a wider audience. Her heroic if imperfect efforts to improve both the quality and quantity of Catholic fiction in America were both admired and controversial in her day and largely forgotten in our own, outside of the College of St. Benedict in St. Joseph, Minnesota, where she taught for decades and where a residential building and an annual literary prize named in her honor keep her memory alive. Sister Mariella did not singlehandedly usher in a golden age of Catholic fiction in the United States in the middle of the twentieth century, but she did perhaps as much as anyone to help bring it about. Her voice, clear and sharp and often very funny, seemed to me to deserve a place at the table in ongoing discussions about Catholic literary fiction.

In expanding that essay into a book, I have continued the story of Sister Mariella's life, criticism, and legacy—especially as they filtered through the writings of her former student Betty Wahl—and have also ventured to include some of my own musings about the theological underpinnings of fiction.

Wahl is mostly remembered today, if she is remembered at all, as the wife of novelist and short-story writer

J. F. Powers. I first came across her work almost twenty years ago, when looking for a project in order to begin a master's degree at the Editorial Institute at Boston University. My prospective advisor at the time, Sir Christopher Ricks, had what I now recall as a literal drawerful of good ideas in his office—ideas which he was too busy to undertake himself and so readily shared with others. Somehow he must have known that I was a churchgoer, although I don't remember ever discussing the subject of religion with him until many years later, and then always to disagree. Christopher rummaged around in his desk for a moment before suggesting I look into the fiction of J. F. Powers.

Powers turned out to be an unsuitable subject for a new scholarly edition, because the New York Review Books Classics series had reissued his work a few years before. But a single line in a biography of Powers—about his wife also being a writer—caught my eye. Soon I found myself in the microfilm room of Mugar Library, reading her *New Yorker* stories. To my pleasant surprise, the stories were funny and good, and to my great good fortune their daughter Katherine A. Powers lived just across the river in Cambridge, Massachusetts.

It was while working on an edition of Betty Wahl's stories for my master's thesis in 2006 that I first learned about Sister Mariella, and it was to Sister Mariella's essays that I returned in 2022 amid ongoing conversations about the state and fate of Catholic literary fiction today. In what looks in retrospect like the work of Providence, the intervening years brought me back to the same Midwestern,

Catholic milieu in which I had been born but not raised, and into which Sister Mariella and Betty Wahl spent much of their writing lives. The intervening years also brought about renewed interest in forgotten Catholic women writers. Wahl's selected stories will soon be available to readers for the first time from Catholic University of America Press.

INTRODUCTION

WHISPER DOWN THE LANE

Textual criticism is a humble and humbling discipline. It takes place behind the scenes, long before a book—whether it's the Bible or *The Adventures of Huckleberry Finn*—lands on bookstore shelves. It involves a great deal of time-intensive, eye-straining, conscientious labor, almost none of which is ultimately visible in the finished product. Yet it's a necessary part of bringing old texts to new readers.

The textual critic is tasked with identifying textual variants, which are differences in phrasing, spelling, punctuation, and other matters both large and small—all the changes that naturally find their way into different copies of a text. The Shakespearean textual critic who wishes to produce a new edition of *King Lear*, for instance, must consult a handful of printed copy-texts, one of which appeared during Shakespeare's lifetime and the rest after. He or she will have no manuscripts—that is, handwritten copy-texts—to look at, because the only examples of Shakespeare's handwriting that we can ascertain are his are a small number of signatures on legal documents. (Though that's perhaps just as well. There are enough irreconcilable differences to be found between the versions of *King Lear* in the First and Second Quartos alone.)

Other writers have left us complete manuscripts in their own handwriting, some with considerably legible script and some with cramped, spidery, impenetrable scrawls. More recent authors have typescripts. The Bible comes to us from a bewildering array of copy-texts, from the Dead Sea Scrolls—written in Hebrew and Aramaic on parchment, papyrus, and copper, and dating back to the time of Christ and earlier—to the Book of Kells, a ninth-century manuscript of the Gospel in Latin, on vellum, famed for its beautiful calligraphy and elaborate illuminations.

All of which is to say that before the reader cracks open a new book, before the bookshop makes a sale, before the warehouse stacks the books on pallets, before the printer prints and binds them—before all this came other hands and other eyes, a long chain of readers and writers (and bards and scribes), whose lives are very far removed from ours today, but whose appreciation of words and stories we share.

When I first encountered textual criticism as an undergraduate, the sheer mess of it both fascinated me and filled me with dismay. Find yourself an image of a stemma—a kind of family-tree for a particular text, which traces its genealogy back through generations of manuscripts—and you'll start to see what I mean. The branches themselves cascade down like willows, beautifully. The whole is lovely to look at. But the overwhelming amount of *work* hidden within that tree (work undertaken by both the scribes who made it the first time and the textual critics who retraced their steps) is daunting.

Daunting, too, is the way that stemmata produce a record not only of individual texts, but of our perennial human propensity for error. Lines of descent within a genealogy are often determined by a shared error or category of errors, and the aim of tracing the family tree back to its roots is usually to pinpoint an original copy-text. That is to say, the earliest known copy-of-a-text and, consequently, the version that had the fewest opportunities for mistakes to be introduced to it by faulty human hands and eyes and minds.

Now, though, I find something touching in this arrangement—in the messy, fallible, and convoluted paths by which culture, tradition, and stories are preserved and passed on. On some level, it's all been one giant version of the children's game "telephone" or "whisper down the lane," going back four thousand years to the invention of the alphabet and beyond. Viewed in this light, it's hardly a wonder that mistakes have been introduced along the way. The real wonder might actually be that the signal, faint or confused though it can become at times, has not disappeared completely into silence or noise.

The image of culture as a children's game writ large, with each player likely to introduce some idiosyncratic mishearing or misspeaking along the way, also shows that nothing is monolithic. Not *King Lear*, not the Bible, and certainly not literature or theology or any other discipline as a whole. What looks solid and complete at first glance brims with complexity and uncertainty on closer inspection.

This system of epistemological fragments and intimations is evidently an intrinsic part of life here below, according to St. Paul. "For now we see through a glass, darkly; but then face to face," he writes: "Now I know in part; but then shall I know even as also I am known" (1 Cor 13:12). On earth one only ever arrives, even in the best-case scenario, at a partial truth. But our dim vision and incomplete knowledge are not necessarily reasons to despair. Elsewhere St. Paul encourages us to boast of our human weaknesses, for in them God's "power is made perfect" (2 Cor 12:9).

It gives me hope to think that thousands upon thousands of overlapping texts, stories, and conversations—each wrong in a slightly different way—might not be a futile mess after all. They might actually be part of God's patient, providential plan for humanity. An invitation to humility, cooperation, and grace.

This book thus begins with an awareness of just how much effort it takes to give even the smallest branch or the tiniest leaf on the tree of knowledge its due. It does not purport to offer *the* theology of fiction, although I would be grateful if a colleague in a department of philosophy or theology or literature were inspired to take up that pursuit. It offers instead *a* theology of fiction—one particular understanding of fiction's theological dimensions, as transmitted through one small branch of a much larger tree. In this instance, there is no prelapsarian urtext to be sought, though there may well be mistakes both inherited and generated by me.

The understanding of fiction outlined here is at heart a sacramental, incarnational one. It is rooted in the Catholic belief that creation and its creatures emanate from God, and that therefore they can speak to us of God—if only we know how to listen and how to look. In this understanding, physical reality contains hints of the metaphysical reality from which it springs and toward which it points. The individual who can see these connections between the perceptible world and the imperceptible world to come— which have the character of metaphor at some times and are transfigured into the thing itself at others—is an individual endowed with what David Tracy has called "the analogical imagination."[1] I first encountered the idea of the analogical imagination from reading Flannery O'Connor, who encountered it from reading St. Augustine.[2] And so on down the lane.

---

1. David Tracy, *The Analogical Imagination: Christian Theology and the Culture of Pluralism* (Chestnut Ridge, PA: Crossroad, 1981).

2. O'Connor writes: "St. Augustine wrote that the things of the world pour forth from God in a double way: intellectually into the minds of the angels and physically into the world of things. To the person who believes this—as the western world did up until a few centuries ago—this physical, sensible world is good because it proceeds from a divine source. The artist usually knows this by instinct; his senses, which are used to penetrating the concrete, tell him so." The role of the novelist, she continues, and of any other artist, is to penetrate "the concrete world in order to find at its depths the image of its source, the image of ultimate reality." Flannery O'Connor, "Novelist and Believer," in *Mystery and Manners: Occasional Prose*, ed. Sally and Robert Fitzgerald (New York: Farrar, Straus and Giroux, 1970), 157.

Belief in a world whose physical properties are created, ennobled, and transcended by God is not a new idea. What Sister Mariella Gable, O.S.B., did was to apply this vision of the world to fictional worlds in a twentieth-century American context, and to use it as a clarion call for Catholic writers to write more and write better. In her teaching, her anthologies, and her literary criticism, she championed a form of fiction that concerns itself with the mundane and the miraculous, and perhaps most especially *the miraculous in the mundane*. She insisted on paying attention to humble, concrete particulars—in stories populated by realistic people in recognizable places—without reducing the whole to materialism. The complex reality of creation and of human persons will evade every attempt to take its full measure. She worked hard to find the best examples of such fiction, and to envision a new form of Catholic fiction that she felt was desperately needed but did not yet exist.

Sister Mariella's insistence on combining realistic characterization and settings with a respect for mystery fell on particularly fertile ground with Betty Wahl. Born in 1924, Wahl was a student at the College of St. Benedict in St. Joseph, Minnesota, where Sister Mariella taught for decades. Wahl was twenty-eight years her junior. After graduating, she continued to be guided by Sister Mariella, who praised Wahl's attempts at a semi-autobiographical first novel and even used it to play matchmaker, sending the manuscript to another promising young Catholic writer, J. F. Powers. Powers liked the novel—and its writer, well enough to marry her. The two went on to have five children, and raised their family half in Minnesota and half in Ireland. Both locales provided settings for their fiction.

Another young writer, Flannery O'Connor, born a year after Wahl, admired Sister Mariella's essays from afar. O'Connor, it hardly needs to be said, absorbed their lessons thoroughly. Hers is now a household name in Catholic fiction, and her short stories have become classics of the genre. In her essays, O'Connor articulates something very close to Sister Mariella's ideas about fiction. The Catholic writer's task, according to O'Connor, is to activate the reader's analogical imagination by "looking for one image that will connect or combine or embody two points; one is a point in the concrete, and the other is a point not visible to the naked eye, but believed in by him"—the writer—"firmly, just as real to him, really, as the one that everybody sees."[3] This "realism of distances," she argues, is "a matter of seeing near things with their extensions of meaning and thus of seeing far things close up" and a mode of contemporary "prophecy."[4]

O'Connor, like Wahl, wrote fiction closely modeled on the people and places she knew best, in her case the rural American South. She and Sister Mariella spoke in person at least once, at Marillac College in 1961.[5] But they mostly

---

3. Flannery O'Connor, "Some Aspects of the Grotesque in Southern Fiction," in *Mystery and Manners: Occasional Prose*, ed. Sally and Robert Fitzgerald (New York: Farrar, Straus and Giroux, 1970), 42.

4. O'Connor, "The Grotesque in Southern Fiction," 44.

5. Flannery O'Connor to "A." [Betty Hester], 11 November 1961, In *The Habit of Being: The Letters of Flannery O'Connor*, ed. Sally Fitzgerald (New York: Vintage, 1979), 453.

developed their overlapping visions of what Catholic fiction should be remotely, through the medium of print, by reading each other's work and writing letters.

Which brings us to one final observation about the literary game of "whisper down the lane." Namely, that this version of "telephone" is also a game of "television." Both words share the Greek prefix *tēle*, meaning "far off." One has a Greek suffix, *phōnē* (meaning "sound" or "voice"), and the other a Latin one, *visio* (from *videre*, "to see"). The kind of "sight at a distance" made possible by a work of fiction means that images which captured the imaginations of Sister Mariella, Wahl, and O'Connor have somehow captured my imagination, too. Without ever meeting any of these three women, I have miraculously benefitted from seeing through their eyes.

My hope now is that readers who are not in the habit of turning to literature in their leisure time might be inspired to pick up a novel or a short story to see firsthand how fiction brings the mind's image-making capacity whirring to life. Or perhaps my hope is that readers who are already in the habit of reading literature might begin to see how, as a friend in graduate school once pointed out, the work of reading, teaching, and writing about fiction is—at the deepest level, if one chooses to engage with it—soul-work. Or perhaps my hope is that somewhere a tired reader (and, as Flannery O'Connor said, "they are all tired") will be lifted up, and made to remember that even if standardized tests, culture wars, and ideological fervor have turned literature into a valley of dry bones—well, even then, we have reason to hope that the God who breathed new life into Ezekiel's vision will breathe new life into our own brittle fragments today.

PROPHET AND PIONEER

Mary Margaret Gable was born in 1898 in rural St. Croix Falls, Wisconsin.[6] In 1915, she entered the novitiate of St. Benedict's Convent, taking the name Sister Mariella, O.S.B. (Ordo Sancti Benedicti). Her promise as a teacher must have been apparent early on because in 1918 she was sent to Bismarck, North Dakota, to help open a new high school. There, she taught all subjects in the ninth and tenth grades, including Latin, English, algebra, geometry, history, typing, and shorthand.[7]

Afterward Sister Mariella spent several years teaching at her alma mater, St. Benedict's Academy, while working toward her bachelor's degree in English at the nearby College of St. Benedict. After receiving her BA in 1925, she joined the college's faculty. Within a decade, Sister Mariella had earned two further degrees in English: an MA from the University of Minnesota—completed through summer programs and correspondence courses squeezed in around her own teaching—and a PhD, which

---

6. The phrase "prophet and pioneer" comes from the introduction to a collection of Sister Mariella Gable's essays edited by Sister Nancy Hynes. I have relied on this volume for nearly all biographical details relating to Sister Mariella's life and for many of her essays. See Nancy Hynes, O.S.B., Introduction to *The Literature of Spiritual Values and Catholic Fiction*, by Mariella Gable, O.S.B., ed. Nancy Hynes (Lanham, MD: University Press of America, 1996), xvii.

7. Hynes, Introduction, xx.

she began at Columbia University and finished at Cornell, after transferring to study with the famed Dante scholar Lane Cooper. Doctorate in hand, Sister Mariella returned to the College of St. Benedict in 1934 to chair the English department.

In an autobiographical essay, Sister Mariella recalled that her transition to religious life had been challenging: "To one so young, so high-spirited, and so accustomed to the free run of woods, hills, and streams, the discipline of the novitiate was difficult."[8] Returning from three years of intellectual pursuits in New York seems to have put her under a similar strain—largely because she couldn't bear to give up those pursuits, even as she took on her old responsibilities as a sister and teacher, and added new ones as department head. She was plagued by abdominal pain, eventually diagnosed as diverticulitis, and recurrent bouts of insomnia and what would now likely be called depression and anxiety. These symptoms were serious enough to land her in the hospital on several occasions, beginning the year after she returned to St. Benedict's. In August 1944, she wrote to a friend, "If I never exhaust myself, I need never get these attacks. The doctor says to keep my sugar up and stay within my limitations."[9]

Her literary output between 1938 and 1950 shows her inability to heed this advice. *Blind Man's Stick*, a book of poems, was published in 1938. Afterward came two anthologies: *Great Modern Catholic Short Stories* in 1942

---

8. Quoted in Hynes, Introduction, xx.

9. Mariella Gable to Roberta Westkaemper, August 1944; quoted in Hynes, Introduction, xix.

(reprinted as *They Are People* in 1944) and *Our Father's House* in 1945. Then a collection of her essays intended for schoolteachers, *This is Catholic Fiction*, in 1948. A third anthology, *Many-Colored Fleece*, appeared in 1950.

Her anthologies helped to put American writers like J. F. Powers and Flannery O'Connor on the map. They also introduced Irish writers including Mary Lavin, Bryan MacMahon, Frank O'Connor, and Seán O'Faoláin to American audiences for the first time. Her criticism insisted that Catholic writers are issued no exemptions for their piety, but must instead be held to the highest standards of quality, craft, and excellence. On this subject, she cited T. S. Eliot approvingly: "The greatness of literature cannot be determined solely by literary standards; though we must remember that whether it is literature or not can be determined only by literary standards."

At the same time, Sister Mariella threw herself into teaching the craft of writing after another nun asked why the college never won any writing awards. "The question," she recalled, "filled me with rage."[10] She set her sights on the most prestigious prize she could find, an annual creative writing contest sponsored by *The Atlantic Monthly*, and within the next few years her students had won half a dozen honorable mentions and twice taken the top prize.[11]

---

10. Kristin Malloy, O.S.B., "Sister Mariella Gable's Life Was Spent Spying on Heaven: A Eulogy," March 24, 1985, College of St. Benedict Archives.

11. Malloy, "Spying on Heaven." A full list of prize winners is given in Hynes, Introduction, xliii n46.

These strenuous efforts attracted both approbation and controversy. The years of Sister Mariella's greatest productivity were also years of poor health and of friction with local bishops. A dustup over her first anthology is illustrative of the resistance she sometimes encountered. Sister Mariella had protested the publisher's choice of title, writing to Frank Sheed, "You can't possibly use *Great Modern Catholic Short Stories* because the book isn't that. It is just one small section of the whole." But Sheed and his co-publisher Maisie Ward overruled her and even advertised it as their Catholic Book of the Month. Soon enough, a censorious priest circulated a pamphlet decrying the book. Privately, Bishop Joseph Busch of the Diocese of St. Cloud told Sister Mariella that the attack "called forth nothing but sympathy." But he also told several local priests that he "had not seen the manuscript"—thereby giving a false impression that she had not sought his imprimatur—and he did nothing to clear up the confusion that ensued.[12]

This kerfuffle put Sister Mariella under a cloud and likely paved the way for later misunderstandings of her work, including, most dramatically, a row over the inclusion of *The Catcher in the Rye* on a recommended reading list in 1958, which led to her exile from St. Benedict's. Although Sister Mariella was vindicated in the end—she taught elsewhere while away, and was able to return to St. Benedict's four years later and retire as professor emerita in 1973—she was, like most prophets, occasionally without honor in her own country.

---

12. Hynes, Introduction, xxviii.

WHAT CATHOLIC FICTION
ISN'T—AND *IS*

The alarm occasioned by Sheed and Ward's mislead-
ing title, discouraging as it was, apparently prompted
Sister Mariella to think deeply about what it would mean
to label a book *Great Modern Catholic Fiction*—and mean
it. In the introduction to her first anthology, Sister Mariella made no attempt to define Catholic fiction; subsequent
essays and anthologies invariably begin with a definition of
this term.

Instead, her earliest motivations had to do with quality.
"God doesn't like crap in art," was J. F. Powers's preferred
formulation, and at times Sister Mariella could be nearly
as blunt. She disliked the magazines she called "Catholic
pulps" and "Catholic slicks" for their "deplorably low" level
of literary craftsmanship, their sensationalism, and their
unrealistic depictions of an idealized—and often bowd-
lerized—faith.[13] Just as women's magazines "consistently
print happy-ending stories that glorify romantic love," she
wrote in 1942,

> the Catholic magazines patronize the same mental-
> ity, with a subtle philosophy of life conspicuously
> more harmful. They seem to say: "If you say your

13. Mariella Gable, O.S.B., "Personality and Catholic Fiction"
[Introduction to *Our Father's House*], in *The Literature of Spiritu-
al Values and Catholic Fiction* (Lanham, MD: University Press of
America, 1996), 23.

prayers (especially if they are repeated nine successive days), if you are good and do the right things, then you shall have a job, succeed in your ambitions, be crowned with the good things of this world"—a kind of back-stairs entrance to materialism, particularly enticing because its easy steps are padded and comfortable with a righteous piety.[14]

To "pour out miracles, three for a cent, cheaper than dirt" made for bad art, in her view.[15] And to "make prayer a means to material satisfactions, as if they were the end of all things to be desired"—in the process doing away with the Church's "teaching on the mystery of suffering," which is "the recipe for the only real happy ending there is"— made for bad theology.[16]

Her first anthology was a rebuke to such presumably well-intentioned, but artistically deficient, stories. In it, Sister Mariella gathered short fiction about priests, nuns, and monks that did away with the "artificial requirements of plot and the pyrotechnics of the O. Henry surprise ending" and instead embraced a quiet realism inspired by Anton Chekhov.[17] Chekhov, she wrote in the introduction,

14. Mariella Gable, O.S.B., "Introduction to *Great Modern Catholic Short Stories*," in *The Literature of Spiritual Values and Catholic Fiction* (Lanham, MD: University Press of America, 1996), 12.

15. Gable, "Personality and Catholic Fiction," 23.

16. Gable, "Personality and Catholic Fiction," 23.

17. Gable, "Introduction to *Great Modern Catholic Short Stories*," 10.

pointed out that people do not go to the North Pole and fall off icebergs; they go to offices, quarrel with their wives, and eat cabbage soup. Similarly, nuns, monks, and priests are not seduced; they teach rapid addition to children in parochial schools, drink the proverbially bad coffee brewed in monastery kitchens, and are occasionally jealous of each other. Thus they are depicted in the contemporary short story.[18]

Hence her preferred title for the collection, *They Are People*: "normal, intelligent persons doing normal, intelligent work."[19]

By gathering these stories—some of which were written by Catholic writers but "scattered to the four winds" (appearing in better-paying secular publications where her target audience might never see them), and others not written by Catholics at all—Sister Mariella wanted to elevate the tastes of Catholic readers by showing them what fiction about Catholic life could and should look like. She also issued her first clarion call to Catholic writers, suggesting that "something of the delicate feeling for truth represented in the present volume" could be useful for illustrating "the life of the spirit," whose workings are "for the most part revealed only obliquely."[20] In his review

---

18. Gable, "Introduction to *Great Modern Catholic Short Stories*," 11.

19. Gable, "Introduction to *Great Modern Catholic Short Stories*," 10.

20. Gable, "Introduction to *Great Modern Catholic Short Stories*," 14.

of the book, Francis X. Connolly, S.J., then chair of the English department at Fordham University, called it "peppery," "provocative," and "explosive enough 'to blow up many a peaceful parish circle.'"[21]

Sister Mariella's earliest, inchoate definition of Catholic fiction was thus a negative one: it wasn't what had passed for Catholic fiction in America in the early decades of the twentieth century. For a variety of reasons, she felt that Catholic literature had not yet come into its own, especially in the United States. By the time Sister Mariella started her work as an editor and critic in the 1940s, the Catholic Revival—which had begun in France and England in the middle of the nineteenth century—had achieved "perfection" (in her view) in poetry, apologetics, and philosophy. Behind them, she noted, "fiction lags conspicuously." To her this seemed a shame, not least because "the number of persons who read fiction is a few thousand times greater than the number of persons who read nonfiction or poetry. Furthermore, the tale or novel has a power to move people" as even the most brilliant philosophy and poetry do not.[22]

Other critics have confirmed Sister Mariella's judgment. In *Testing the Faith: The New Catholic Fiction in America* (1992), Anita Gandolpho refers to the period from 1900 to 1950 as an "Age of Innocence" in which

---

21. Quoted in Hynes, Introduction, xxviii.

22. Mariella Gable, O.S.B., "Catholic Life and Catholic Fiction," in *The Literature of Spiritual Values and Catholic Fiction* (Lanham, MD: University Press of America, 1996), 2.

Catholic writers were driven by "didacticism" rather than literary quality.[23] Jean Kellogg's *The Vital Tradition: The Catholic Novel in a Period of Convergence* (1970) suggests that the pragmatic nature of clerical life in America may have slowed the development of Catholic fiction in the United States. The American priest "was from the beginning, typically, a man of action," she writes: "a missionary in frontier territories, an educator of previously uneducated immigrant masses, and a builder of schools and churches, who battled for his parishioners against exploiters of the immigrant poor."[24] The realities of a demanding parish life "made higher studies almost impossible," as evidenced by the low enrollments at Catholic University of America in its early years. And the American church made a virtue of necessity, prioritizing practical matters over the exploration of theological complexities.[25] Kellogg's study of American Catholic authors begins with Powers and O'Connor, and she suggests that the reason "that Catholic novels begin so late in America is probably due to the low regard in which American Catholics for so long held the life of the intellect."[26]

Looking at the matter from a different angle, we find that the trajectory of American literature more broadly tells a different—but related—story. A survey course

---

23. Quoted in Hynes, Introduction, xl.

24. Jean Kellogg, *The Vital Tradition: The Catholic Novel in a Period of Convergence* (Chicago: Loyola University Press, 1970), 151.

25. Kellogg, *The Vital Tradition*, 164.

26. Kellogg, *The Vital Tradition*, 165.

on American literature will never be short on high-quality fiction, but if you take one you'll be hard-pressed to find much overt faith after the Puritan sermons. Nathaniel Hawthorne was nearly alone in his attempts to make room for supernatural elements in American fiction, and he did so self-consciously. He knew that his readers would expect novels to "aim at a very minute fidelity, not merely to the possible, but to the probable and ordinary course of man's experience."[27] So he called his works of long fiction "romances" instead, to leave himself recourse to the extraordinary and the miraculous: mesmerism and curses, metamorphosis, celestial omens, and physical manifestations of sin and other spiritual realities. After Hawthorne's death, Henry James dismissed the romance as an inferior genre, and nearly a century and a half later, it has yet to recover. Today, the novelistic descendants of James are as numberless as the stars, but Hawthorne has—apart from perhaps William Faulkner and Toni Morrison—almost no heirs.

Again, it's worth asking not just whither Catholic fiction in this country, but also whence. The 1950s and 1960s saw Catholic, Protestant, and Jewish writers fêted by the literary world, but to take that period as a baseline for narratives of decline (or a lack of decline) is somewhat strange. That period may actually be the exception that proves the rule, namely that high-quality fiction and

27. Nathaniel Hawthorne, Preface, *The House of Seven Gables*, with an introduction by Denis Donoghue (Cambridge, MA: Belknap Press, 2009), 1.

fiction about faith have mostly run on parallel tracks in American literary history. Never before the middle of the twentieth century did we have such an openly religious moment in "serious" American fiction, and we may never have one again.

WHAT CATHOLIC FICTION *IS*

Closing the gap between fiction of quality and fiction of faith constituted the first part of Sister Mariella's program of reform. The second part involved articulating what would distinguish Catholic fiction of the highest quality from its secular counterparts.

Never an abstract thinker—her favorite word was reportedly "concrete"—Sister Mariella used the image of a bulls-eye in the introduction to her second anthology, *Our Father's House*, to suggest the kind of subjects on which Catholics should train their sights. The outer circle of the target depicts "the local color of Catholic life."[28] Although such fiction was the focus of her first anthology, by 1945 she had deemed it "peripheral."[29] Neither necessary nor sufficient for her definition of Catholic fiction, rich Catholic settings would mostly give Catholic writers the chance "to become adept in our own idiom."[30] The next circle of the bulls-eye dramatizes ethical issues—for instance,

---

28. Gable, "Personality and Catholic Fiction," 22.

29. Gable, "Personality and Catholic Fiction," 22.

30. Gable, "Personality and Catholic Fiction," 22.

birth control or race relations—in a way that aligns with the teachings of the Catholic Church. The center of the target tackles something murkier: the inner workings of the person who desires earnestly to live, though not without struggles and failures, in accordance with Catholic teachings. It might touch on any number of ethical problems—even ones the Church hasn't formally weighed in on—because "these problems become Catholic when treated from a God-centered point of view."[31]

The bulls-eye image illustrates what Sister Mariella loved most about fiction: its special epistemology, its specific form of *knowing through seeing*. But it is unique among her explications in describing the particular subject matter that Catholic fiction ought to cover. The rest of the time she focused on what Catholic fiction ought to *do*.

THE RE-EDUCATION OF LOVE

In *Our Father's House*, Sister Mariella's teleology of Catholic fiction builds on Dietrich von Hildebrand's *Liturgy and Personality*. Hildebrand argues that the formation of Christian personality involves developing an appropriate response to value. "What does it mean to make an appropriate response to value?" Sister Mariella asks, and answers:

---

31. Gable, "Personality and Catholic Fiction," 21.

It means that all the things we can know are ranged in a hierarchy of being, some deserving less love, some more. It means that we strive to give each thing the love it deserves, and that we are done once and for all with the feverish desire merely to be different. It does away with the romantic emphasis upon the ego. It does not ask: how do I feel about clam chowder and Gothic architecture? do I worship baby pandas and regard moral restraint as silly? It molds the classic personality, essentially noble, admirable, and balanced. A classic personality is never absolutely achieved, but the person striving to attain its perfection habitually endeavors to make an appropriate response to value. Appropriate—that which in the hierarchy of being this particular thing deserves.[32]

Nature is clearly good, but it is not the ultimate good. Friendship, too. If we make idols of them, Sister Mariella writes, "if we give more than an appropriate response" to any particular value, "the value itself betrays us"—there are tempests as well as idylls—and we are left frustrated, unfulfilled, and longing for more.[33]

The specifically *Christian* "classic personality" recognizes that God is the ultimate good and feels sympathy for those still searching. Following Étienne Gilson, it believes that "all human love is a love of God unaware of itself," and thus "the question is not how to acquire the love of God,

32. Gable, "Personality and Catholic Fiction," 19.

33. Gable, "Personality and Catholic Fiction," 19.

but rather how to make it fully aware of itself, of its object, and of the way it should bear itself toward this object. In this sense we might say that the only difficulty is the education, or if you prefer it, re-education of love."[34]

The end of Catholic fiction, then, is to bring about this re-education of love, through a slow and imperfect process of conversion meant to take place often in a book's characters but perhaps always in its readers. When the center of the bulls-eye depicts saints—not heavy-hitters like Francis or Anthony, but everyday people striving for holiness—it shows persons who are continually making decisions about what to value.

Any story that truthfully represents value in this way qualifies as Catholic fiction according to Sister Mariella, no matter the denomination of the characters or the author, who may even lack religious faith. Not only this, but negative fiction—fiction that shows what *not* to do or *not* to value, and why—counts, too. In her third anthology, *Many-Colored Fleece*, Sister Mariella included "Missis Flinders," a story by screenwriter Tess Slesinger that is based on the author's experience of having an abortion. "In it," Sister Mariella writes, "a husband and wife have freed themselves from the troubles, expense, and responsibility of parenthood by an abortion. Apparently unhampered by any religious scruples, they suffer frightfully in their subtle contempt of each other."[35] It is a hard story to read even

---

34. Gable, "Personality and Catholic Fiction," 20.

35. Mariella Gable, O.S.B., "Introduction to *Many-Colored Fleece*," in *The Literature of Spiritual Values and Catholic Fiction* (Lanham, MD: University Press of America, 1996), 39.

today, disorienting and devastating as the woman's mind turns in on itself—now angry, now remorseful, now bitterly, ironically nonchalant about what has happened; at once envying and despising the other mothers who share her room at the maternity hospital; silently seething with hatred for her husband. Her loves and wraths alike are disordered and intermixed. Such a "story of failure," Sister Mariella writes, "is often like the hole in the wall, without which we could not see the thickness, strength, and solidity of the masonry."[36] Not all stone walls a prison make; some are there to protect, to hold up.

SALVATION AND DAMNATION IN
THE DRAWING ROOM

In the introduction to *Many-Colored Fleece*, Sister Mariella reframes her argument about the *telos* of Catholic fiction, in a way that remains consonant with her earlier discussion of value. For Christians, every choice leads the chooser in one direction or another, toward salvation or damnation. This ability to see *sub specie aeternitatis*—that is, to consider our present reality in relation to the eternal—gives the Catholic writer a broader palette to work from than a secular writer has. It gives him or her access to three dimensions, whereas the writer without faith has only one.

"Even Catholics have wrongly supposed that Catholic fiction is limited, narrow in its subject matter, curbed and

---

36. Gable, "Introduction to *Many-Colored Fleece*," 39.

curtailed in what it may do," Sister Mariella writes. "The fact is: Secular fiction is limited. Catholic fiction is unlimited; it embraces all reality."[37] She explains:

> Fiction is about people. Take any drawing-room full of people. The first reality with which we are confronted is the individuality of all present. God never repeats himself. God manifests something of the mystery of His fecundity as a Creator in the infinite variety of human beings—no two on the face of the earth precisely alike. In our drawing-room are the witty, the depressed, the insecure, the amicable, the lonely, the garrulous, the silent. But one witty person differs from another witty person, one silent man from another inarticulate one as color differs from color. Yet they are all bound by the bond of coloredness—the mystery of the one and the many. Moreover a psychological and social chemistry takes place whereby color fades into color or clashes with it. Traditional fiction has been sociological. It has dealt with the relationship of one human being to another. It has interpreted the many-coloredness of the human beings in society—whether transcending their environment or becoming victims to it. It has dealt with the reality of a material world, and in doing so has projected a fiction of one dimension.[38]

---

37. Gable, "Introduction to *Many-Colored Fleece*," 32.

38. Gable, "Introduction to *Many-Colored Fleece*," 32–33.

Catholic fiction takes into account this psychological and sociological dimension, and adds another. "But there is another reality in that drawing-room," Sister Mariella writes. "Every person present is either in a state of grace or of damnation. In other words, heaven and hell are present in the room. A fiction which extends its boundaries to include this reality is eschatological."[39] It "embraces all planes of reality."[40]

If this sounds like a précis of Flannery O'Connor's account of the Christian novelist as a "realist of distances," it may well be. O'Connor's essay "Some Aspects of the Grotesque in Southern Fiction" was written a decade later, and her letters show that she admired Sister Mariella's criticism.[41]

Sister Mariella singles out Graham Greene's *The Heart of the Matter* for having included just such an eschatological dimension. In it, the protagonist has an extramarital affair and afterwards receives communion in a state of mortal sin. Unable to renounce his mistress or his marriage, and stricken by his own further offense against God, Henry Scobie overdoses on sleeping pills; the novel ends with his wife Louise discussing his apparent suicide with her priest. "People cared tremendously whether Scobie was damned or saved," Sister Mariella writes, with evident delight. "His plight was argued by the literary

39. Gable, "Introduction to *Many-Colored Fleece*," 33.

40. Gable, "Introduction to *Many-Colored Fleece*," 33.

41. O'Connor, "The Grotesque in Southern Fiction," 179.

elite and by callow youth—at cocktail parties, in bars, in monastery parlors, and over Cokes in drugstores."[42]

She observes that medieval allegory had taken just such an interest in eschatological reality—in the ultimate destination of our souls—but in it characters were "only symbols—often dehumanized."[43] What contemporary Catholic writers might do, she suggests, is to build on Greene's work, by continuing to develop forms of fiction that take into account both "spiritual reality" and the concern for "human individuality" that is characteristic of novels.[44]

NEGATIVE FICTION AND THE PSYCHOLOGY OF GOODNESS

By a terrible irony, Sister Mariella noted, goodness is harder to portray on the page than is its lack. "Missis Flinders" and *The Heart of the Matter* are both examples of negative fiction. As for positive fiction, she points the reader to "The Devil in the Desert" by Paul Horgan or "Lions, Harts, and Leaping Does" by J. F. Powers. But most of it has yet to be written.

"The psychology of goodness is very rarely explored with anything like the artistic success that commonly distinguishes the analysis of evil or of spiritual failure," Sister

---

42. Gable, "Introduction to *Many-Colored Fleece*," 33.

43. Gable, "Introduction to *Many-Colored Fleece*," 33.

44. Gable, "Introduction to *Many-Colored Fleece*," 34.

Mariella writes. "St. Augustine remarked in the *City of God*, Book XI, Chapter 9: 'Evil has no positive nature; but the loss of good has received the name evil.' In the art of literature it would seem to be the other way round."[45] Ahead of William Empson, though after Percy Bysshe Shelley, she takes aim at John Milton's *Paradise Lost* as a textbook case of this phenomenon: "Milton meant to argue God's cause, but his devils are magnificent, while God the Father and God the Son talk like two smug Presbyterian ministers sipping tea before a fireplace."[46] More recently, she asserts, "bad Catholic fiction" of the early twentieth century makes virtue unpalatable in a different way, by assuming that "a certain amount of goodness transfers the character from the state of original sin to some Eden-like perfection never seen on land or sea. The presupposition is heretical."[47]

What is needed instead is "plain honesty" about the fact that, here below, good is always mixed with temptation and with failings, even in saints. "Such a fiction will certainly not be dull," she envisions. "For the sharpest conflict in the world begins to take place the moment a soul sets out to seek God in earnest. Self immediately kicks and screams for the center of attention. And if somewhat flouted in the struggle, self-seeking can disguise itself in a million ways to look like God-seeking."[48] And yet some souls persist. In those cases, "What happens between the soul and God?

---

45. Gable, "Introduction to *Many-Colored Fleece*," 36.

46. Gable, "Introduction to *Many-Colored Fleece*," 36.

47. Gable, "Introduction to *Many-Colored Fleece*," 38.

48. Gable, "Introduction to *Many-Colored Fleece*," 37.

Everyone wants to know. But the task of fiction is not only to give the information, but to impart on the level of pure art the vicarious experience."[49]

Sister Mariella hoped to see laypeople lead the way in realizing her vision for a literature of spiritual values. "In 1942 there was every reason to rejoice at the kind of story which appeared in *They Are People*," she wrote, again in the introduction to *Our Father's House*. But by 1950, high-quality stories about clerical life could "be had for a dime a dozen."[50] What lay authors needed to do was stop writing about priests and start chronicling their own experiences, and particularly the increasingly "heroic fortitude" needed to sustain a marriage and to raise a family in modern American culture. In an age that encourages materialism and instant gratification of the ego's every whim, some people still choose to make room for contemplation, for charity, for sanctity—or at least they try to. In their efforts "lies the reality out of which a great and noble fiction might be made."[51]

And if you can't write fiction, she advised, then raise your children steadfastly in the faith. Maybe they will have the gift.

---

49. Gable, "Introduction to *Many-Colored Fleece*," 38.

50. Gable, "Introduction to *Many-Colored Fleece*," 41.

51. Gable, "Introduction to *Many-Colored Fleece*," 42.

THE PARADOX OF CATHOLIC FICTION

Reading Sister Mariella's criticism two generations later, one encounters a stunningly lively voice. She writes with earned confidence and enviable wit; she frequently astonishes with her insight and perspicuity; she is matter-of-fact in her treatment of artistic and theological triumphs and failures alike. But initially her scholarship was met with hostility, at least from some quarters. And, indeed, one definition of paradox is a tenet that runs contrary to received opinion.

PARADOX: AGAINST RECEIVED OPINION

Bishop Busch's coadjutor, Bishop Bartholome, was put off by the Chekhovian realism of her first anthology, *They Are People*, viewing it as proof of Sister Mariella's anticlericalism. It was Bishop Bartholome, and not Bishop Busch, from whom she was required to seek an imprimatur for her second anthology. After a disastrous interview exposed their differing views on the yardstick by which to measure fiction, there followed a year and a half of delays.[52]

On February 13, 1945, Sister Mariella wrote with great relief to Father Vincent J. Flynn, then president of the College of St. Thomas in St. Paul, Minnesota, who had included one of her essays in a textbook he edited. "After seventeen months of grief," she reported, when

---

52. Hynes, Introduction, xxv.

the Diocesan Censor at St. John's Abbey had finished his review, "not a syllable to be changed."[53] But even after that, Bishop Bartholome continued to stall publication by designating another outside reader to review the manuscript. Eventually, Sister Mariella's publisher, Frank Sheed, suggested that he obtain an imprimatur instead from Archbishop Francis Spellman in New York. Sister Mariella agreed and an imprimatur was granted.

Though such an arrangement is permissible by Canon Law, Bishop Bartholome appears to have greatly resented it.[54] More than a decade later, in 1958, when the inclusion of *The Catcher in the Rye* on a suggested reading list for contemporary American literature at the College of St. Benedict raised the ire of a local priest, Bishop Bartholome insisted that the only way to resolve the issue was for Sister Mariella to leave the diocese entirely. A heartbroken letter from Sister Mariella to her superior, Mother Richarda, from June 1958, shows her distress at being exiled. "I cannot tell you how much this decision has cost me," she wrote. "I love St. Benedict's, I love teaching, I love all that I must leave."[55]

Earlier letters testify to the pain she endured during previous periods of forced removal from the College of St. Benedict, to treat her nervous troubles. The summer of 1950 found her at a hospital in Utah staffed by Benedictines and in the care of a Dr. O'Gorman. That fall, she was forced to undergo three months of solitary confinement

---

53. Quoted in Hynes, Introduction, xxvi.

54. Hynes, Introduction, xxxiii.

55. Hynes, Introduction, xxxi.

and a series of shocks—first insulin and then electric—without her permission. "When Dr. O'G was in here today I asked him, just for the record, whether I am sane or insane now," Sister Mariella wrote to Sister Remberta Westkaemper, a dear friend, in November 1950. "He said, 'You are sane, sane as you will ever be.' But am I not, being sane, a free agent with the right to refuse electric shock and solitary confinement? These methods will not help me. Of that I am sure."[56]

The same month saw publication of her third anthology, *Many-Colored Fleece*. The English department at St. Benedict's sent her a congratulatory telegram, but no one at the hospital in Utah mentioned the book on the day of its release. Sister Mariella, writing again to Sister Remberta, called it "the most miserable day of my life."[57] When solitary confinement and shocks did not work, the doctor performed an intraorbital lobotomy, again without consent. He told Sister Mariella of the procedure only three days later.[58]

Her time away from St. Benedict's from 1958 to 1962 was in one sense even more distressing than the questionable medical treatment she received in Utah, because it made Sister Mariella wonder whether she had in fact been "a shade 'too liberal'" in her teaching.[59] But the support she

---

56. Quoted in Hynes, Introduction, xlv n64.

57. 19 November 1950, quoted in Hynes, Introduction, xlv n64.

58. Hynes, Introduction, xxix and xlv nn63–64.

59. Hynes, Introduction, xxxiv; the text in the first set of quotation marks indicates Hynes's words, those inside the inner quotation marks are Sister Mariella's.

received from other Catholic academics, especially Father Harold C. Gardiner, S.J., during this period of exile helped restore her confidence.

After four years of teaching in Colorado, Oregon, and Missouri, and a summer spent studying abroad at the University of Oxford in England, Sister Mariella was able to return to the College of St. Benedict, thanks in part to a new prioress and new coadjutor bishop. But even then, as Sister Nancy Hynes, O.S.B., writes in the introduction to her edited collection of Sister Mariella's essays, "recognition and acceptance abroad did not mean acceptance at home."[60]

The new prioress, Mother Henrita Osendorf, O.S.B., urged Sister Mariella in correspondence to "come home willing to let others champion the cause of certain kinds of literature. Rather than bring up the old problem, it is better to let the matter rest in silence; can you agree with me on this?"[61] The margins of the letter record Sister Mariella's responses: "Rubbish" and "Nuts." But when asked whether she would agree, the marginalia reads, "Of course." Next to Mother Henrita's request that she not "bear a grudge": "Not the least."[62]

Sister Mariella seems to have kept her promise, rendering obedience to her superiors without losing her convictions or her sense of humor. When Sister Kristin Malloy, O.S.B.—a former student of Sister Mariella's who became a treasured colleague in the St. Ben's English

---

60. Hynes, Introduction, xxxv.

61. Hynes, Introduction, xxxv.

62. Quoted in Hynes, Introduction, xxxv.

department—was also turned out over the *Catcher in the Rye* controversy in 1958, Sister Mariella wrote to Father Thomas Egan, "Kristin is expelled, too. Only the Puritans remain."[63]

In Sister Mariella's poor reception from some quarters, we see something of the larger paradox inherent in the Christian faith. The good news is never welcomed by all: some messengers are invited in for dinner and others are greeted by a baying mob; some messages fall on willing ears, others are met with scorn and disbelief. The Christian faith endlessly inverts and subverts worldly logic and worldly expectations. It makes the first last and the last first; it dines with the disreputable and decries the establishment; it brings those on the periphery of society into the center. It says that money and might are useless, and that treasures must be stored inwardly and immaterially, where no moth or rust or thief may go. To take the Christian faith seriously—and the revealed wisdom on which it is built—is to be kept continually on one's guard and on one's toes.

Indeed, what distinguishes the genius from the apostle, according to Søren Kierkegaard, is the fact that the latter's message can never quite be squared with worldly thinking. Genius may "have something new to bring forth, but what it brings forth disappears again as it becomes assimilated by the human race," he writes. "The Apostle has, paradoxically, something new to bring, the newness

---

63. Mariella Gable to Thomas Egan, 14 August 1958. Quoted in Hynes, Introduction, xxxiii.

of which, precisely because it is essentially paradoxical, and not an anticipation of the development of the race, always remains."[64] There is a reason that we can learn about gravity once in our schooldays and never doubt its existence again, but we must be reminded of the Resurrection weekly, and even then it continues to slip out of view.

It makes sense that even well-intentioned people of faith, who must after all live in the world, can be tempted to sink into what Walker Percy calls the "everydayness" of their own lives. It is terribly easy to resist rather than welcome, the strange, wonderful, and endlessly unsettling newness of God's grace, Christ's peace, and the Holy Spirit's counsel. For everyone "reverently, passionately waiting / for the miraculous birth," in W. H. Auden's memorable formulation, "there must always be / Children who did not specially want it to happen, skating / On a pond at the edge of the wood."[65]

So, too, for every one person eager to think through with Sister Mariella and her spiritual descendants ways in which contemporary culture might be renewed by the Holy Spirit (acting at least in part through fiction writers), there will be many others who see no need.

---

64. Søren Kierkegaard, "Of the Difference Between the Genius and the Apostle," in *The Present Age: On the Death of Rebellion*, trans. Alexander Dru and intro. Walter Kaufman (New York: Harper, 2010), 67.

65. W. H. Auden, "Musée des Beaux Arts," in *The Norton Anthology of Poetry*, Shorter Fifth Edition, ed. Margaret Ferguson, Mary Jo Salter, and Jon Stallworthy (New York: Norton, 2005), 939.

Paradox has another meaning, too. It can refer to a statement or proposition that seems absurd or self-contradictory but could in fact be true. Sister Mariella offered just such a proposition—or rather a series of propositions—in her last systematic treatment of Catholic fiction, an essay on the Catholic novel in 1962. That was the year that Walker Percy's *The Moviegoer* won the National Book Award for fiction; the following year the prize would go to J. F. Powers for *Morte D'Urban*.

Accordingly, Sister Mariella begins on a triumphant note. "The output of competent Catholic novels is so impressive in quantity and quality that, at the present time, it is regarded by secular critics as a badge of distinction for an author to be designated as a Catholic novelist," she writes.[66] (As ever, she excludes *in*competent novels from consideration: "for, unless a work is first a piece of art, it cannot qualify as a piece of Catholic art."[67])

But she also acknowledges ongoing disagreements about what exactly constitutes a Catholic novel. "This disagreement," she writes, "is easily understood when one realizes that it takes its rise, as do most disputes, from an overemphasis on one part of a complex truth. To bring into focus the whole of the truth about Catholic fiction, it

---

66. Mariella Gable, O.S.B., "The Novel," in *The Literature of Spiritual Values and Catholic Fiction* (Lanham, MD: University Press of America, 1996), 51.

67. Gable, "The Novel," 51.

is necessary to keep in mind three facts."[68] These facts she presents, rather koan-like, as follows:

> Each one of the following statements is true; without a grasp of their coexistence, no satisfactory definition of Catholic fiction can be formulated.

1. Strictly speaking, Catholic fiction does not exist.

2. All the great literature in the world is Catholic fiction.

3. Fiction which artistically communicates through the use of Catholic symbols something of the spiritual and moral mystery of the human condition may properly be designated Catholic fiction.[69]

Sister Mariella's explication of these "facts" is itself somewhat cryptic.

She begins by defining "fiction" in this instance as any "story" that "explores the mystery of the human condition for the purpose of giving pleasure."[70] A story, she continues, reveals its wisdom through concrete particulars. In doing so, it gives insight into human life that "no abstraction, no recounting of history, no nonfiction writing of any sort can communicate."[71]

---

68. Gable, "The Novel," 52.

69. Gable, "The Novel," 52–53.

70. Gable, "The Novel," 53.

71. Gable, "The Novel," 53.

Because any story filled with concrete particulars necessarily shows only a partial slice of the human condition, this partiality puts it at odds with the world-encompassing elements of Catholicism, whose etymology can be traced to the Greek words *kata* ("in respect of") and *holos* ("the whole"), hence *katholikos* (meaning "universal"). Such narrowing, she argues, following literary critic Allen Tate, forces the author to become a kind of *de facto* heretic: "for heresy is precisely the giving of excessive emphasis to any one truth to the neglect of counterbalancing truths."[72] Taking into account fiction's heretical inclinations in this sense, as well as its ability to convey insight into the mystery of the human condition from religious traditions other than Christianity, Sister Mariella concludes that "it is true, therefore, that Catholic fiction is simply fiction. And those who insist that there is no such thing as Catholic fiction certainly have grounds for their position."[73]

Conversely, she grants that those on the other side of the debate have an equal right to claim that "all the great fiction in the world is Catholic fiction."[74] Here, she invokes John Henry Newman's "pronouncement" that "by Catholic literature is not to be understood a literature which treats exclusively or primarily of Catholic matters, or Catholic doctrine, controversy, history, persons, or politics, but it includes all subjects of literature whatever, treated as a

---

72. Gable, "The Novel," 53–54.

73. Gable, "The Novel," 54.

74. Gable, "The Novel," 54.

Catholic would treat them, and as he only can treat them."[75] Following this view, Sister Mariella argues that fiction which does not engage with the eschatological dimension of the human condition cannot be great fiction. Her second statement isn't concerned with novelists' "subject matter," nor with "the *particular symbolism*" they use to convey it, but rather with "the depth and insight of their spiritual vision."[76] Great fiction cannot remain at the surface of human experience; it must get to the heart of the matter, to the way human beings straddle time and eternity. Great fiction must concern itself with—and reveal to readers—exactly the sort of eternal truths that have been preserved by the Catholic Church, though it presents them differently.

Her third statement Sister Mariella clarifies by saying that the "communication of spiritual and moral insight" is essential to her definition of Catholic fiction, while the "use of Catholic symbols" is merely accidental.[77] Here, she cites John's Gospel—"If any one love me, he will keep my word, and my Father will love him, and we will come to him, and will make our abode with him" (14:23)—apparently to suggest that the Holy Spirit will land on whomever He pleases.[78]

---

75. Quoted in Gable, "The Novel," 55.

76. Gable, "The Novel," 56; emphasis in original.

77. Gable, "The Novel," 57.

78. Gable, "The Novel," 56.

So it transpires that Sister Mariella, one of the most astute critics of Catholic fiction that the United States has produced, was ready to admit that debates about its definition, parameters, and even its existence are likely to go on indefinitely.

COMEDY'S CORRECTIVE VALUE

Many-Colored Fleece was to be Sister Mariella's last anthology. But when it was published in 1950 she was only halfway through her teaching career. Though she wrote less, she continued to review books and to speak at conferences and other engagements, while developing a reputation as an expert on Flannery O'Connor's fiction and the theology of Pierre Teilhard de Chardin.[79] Even after she retired from the College of St. Benedict in 1973, she continued for several years to offer her famous course on Dante—beloved by decades of students—to St. Ben's alumnae.[80] Sister Mariella marked her Diamond Jubilee in 1977, celebrating sixty years of professed religious life. She died at St. Scholastica Convent, in St. Cloud, Minnesota, in 1985.[81]

THE "IS-OUGHT" PREREQUISITE

One later paper by Sister Mariella provides a jumping off point for considerations of how fiction's eschatological dimension may relate to genre.

In "Prose Satire and the Modern Christian Temper," which was published in the *American Benedictine Review* in 1960, Sister Mariella takes as her starting point the old

---

79. Hynes, Introduction, xxxv, xxxvi.

80. Hynes, Introduction, xxxvi.

81. Hynes, Introduction, xxxvi.

saw that the enemy of my enemy is my friend. Though Aldous Huxley dabbled in Eastern religions and mysticism and George Orwell rejected faith of every kind, she enlists them to the cause of the Catholic Church. What both writers do effectively (if unwittingly), she argues, is to depict vividly the dangers of replacing older, religious forms of group identity—based on doctrines like the Body of Christ or concepts such as the divine right of kings—with newer, secular, solely political ones. In Huxley's *Brave New World* (1932) and Orwell's *Nineteen Eighty-Four* (1949), the "omnipotent State unchecked by any power" quickly erodes individual freedom and normative morality.[82] "Both satires," writes Sister Mariella, regard the "loss of freedom as the major calamity that could befall a human being" and both "rebel" against the "operational determinism" of totalitarian governments.[83]

"Whether one contemplates in either of the satiric allegories the spectacle of an omnipotent state ruining human beings by excessive comfort or excessive torture," she continues, "the prognostic is terrifying. Evil stalks the world. It cannot be conquered except by first safeguarding the individual."[84] Orwell emphasizes the state's capacity for "excessive torture"—that is, its ultimate grounding in coercion through a monopoly on the legitimate use of

82. Mariella Gable, O.S.B., "Prose Satire and the Modern Christian Temper," in *The Literature of Spiritual Values and Catholic Fiction* (Lanham, MD: University Press of America, 1996), 144.

83. Gable, "Prose Satire," 144; second quote is Martin Kessler, quoted in Gable, "Prose Satire," 145.

84. Gable, "Prose Satire," 146.

physical force. Two World Wars had made painfully apparent the potential for monstrous overreach by governments which could, through a system of national conscription devised during the French Revolution and later copied by other nations, compel their citizens to kill and be killed. Huxley's dystopia of "excessive comfort," by contrast, ponders whether an interior kind of conscription into a more insidious new order had begun in the twentieth century as well—one that values the individual merely as a consumer of goods and entertainment, rather than as a moral agent in a coherent social world.

Both novels present these dangers to readers in the form of well-wrought, vivid, vicarious human experience, which makes them good examples of "negative fiction." But neither author is able to imagine any kind of solution that would prevent the contemporary nation-state from abusing its power. Their inability to do, Sister Mariella suggests, is tied to their lack of faith. "The two satires under discussion," she writes, "show the horror of the omnipotent State unchecked by any power. They do not suggest any power able to prevent the State from abusing its omnipotence, for there is none other than the Church."[85]

Two other satirists whom Sister Mariella considers in the essay tackle the second, interior kind of conscription emerging in the twentieth century, the one that subtly elides value judgments and normative morality. But for these two writers—both Catholic—the prognostic isn't terrifying. Instead, it's more likely darkly funny.

---

85. Gable, "Prose Satire," 144.

Muriel Spark's *Memento Mori* (1959) and Aubrey Menen's *The Stumbling Stone* (1949) each skewer the disappearance from academic pursuits and social reform of value judgments grounded in the nature of reality. Sister Mariella argued in her earlier work that a proper determination of and response to value is essential to human flourishing. Spark and Menen examine what happens when human development is understood differently, and when normative morality is deemed nonexistent or irrelevant to human betterment.

In *Memento Mori*, sociologist Alec Warner amasses reams of data about the elderly, only to lose it all in a fire. As his papers burn, the thought suddenly comes to him that "the human is indeed different from that which can be measured, charted, or tabulated." Menen suggests that the appeal of human metrics like the ones Warner futilely gathers has little to do with their accuracy or utility, and much to do with the evasion of duty they permit: "Instead of the agony of saving our souls, we prefer the pleasure of saving other people's. They save us the trouble of looking into our own hearts."[86]

But reducing our understanding of human persons to what can be empirically observed and measured in this way is actually as vexed as inferences moving in the other direction have been sometimes thought to be. In *A Treatise of Human Nature* (1739), David Hume observed that it isn't clear from a purely rational and empirical point of view how what *ought to be* derives from what merely

---

86. Quoted in Gable, "Prose Satire," 149, 148.

is—and he proposed, as a consequence, with more than a grain of irony and illogic, that we *ought* to disregard the existence of *oughts* until such a link can be discovered. Since then, empiricist philosophers following Hume have tried to find a way around this "is–ought problem" (also called Hume's Law). Two centuries later, their efforts to discern an empirical basis for morality—one that is independent of a teleological understanding of nature—have yet to succeed.[87]

Spark and Menen show in their fiction that what has so far failed in theory is doomed to fail in practice as well. Any attempt to comprehend human experience by examining what merely *is* and ignoring what *ought to be*—and, consequently, any attempt to respond to problems produced by a misunderstanding of value with solely descriptive, factual solutions—is likely to meet with similarly disappointing results. And not only because focusing on someone else's *is* can indeed be an excellent way to avoid paying attention to your own *oughts*.

For writers who believe, in the words of the Nicene Creed, in God the Father, "maker of heaven and earth, all things visible and *invisible*," the occluded nature of the hinge linking *is* and *ought* is not a "problem" in need of a solution.[88] The precise mechanism linking our physical bodies and our intellects is likewise hidden, but that

---

87. See James Davison Hunter and Paul Nedelisky, *Science and the Good: The Tragic Quest for the Foundations of Morality* (New Haven: Yale University Press, 2018).

88. Emphasis added.

doesn't stop us from walking and talking. Lived experience provides ample proof of correspondences between physical and metaphysical reality; and, where gaps remain, we may see not problems to be solved, but mysteries to be accepted on faith.

Certain genres of fiction actually demand the kind of stereoscopic, ironic vision made possible by the differences between what *is* and what *ought to be*. And these genres require an "is–ought" distinction regardless of the author's own deeply held metaphysical views, or lack thereof. Satire is one such genre. Comedy is another.

COMEDY AS CORRECTIVE

Although Sister Mariella never fully elaborated on the relationship between comedy and the Christian temper, she did include a paragraph on "the place of humor in Catholic fiction" in the introduction to *Many-Colored Fleece*:

> Is humor an element that must of necessity be part of Catholic fiction? Perhaps yes. The incongruous incites to laughter. In spite of people's high dedication as children of God, they still remain weak and human and full of vagaries. They are like kings and queens in royal robes who seven times a day slip on the banana peel of their weak human nature. Viewed from one angle their failure is uproariously funny. From another it is immeasurably serious and gives a resonance and spiritual significance to one's concept of human nature. Only a noble view

of human nature can be humorous. There is nothing funny about an art which depicts human beings
as falling off the floor.[89]

Sister Mariella's views here are consonant with a larger intellectual tradition called the incongruity theory of
humor.

The incongruity theory of humor was first formu-
lated by James Beattie in 1779. Before that, laughter was
primarily believed to be the result of discovering and to
some extent gloating over another's blemishes and character defects. The Roman word for this superiority theory of
humor, *ridiculus*, has survived nearly intact to the present
day. What James Beattie, along with other eighteenth-cen-
tury philosophers including Francis Hutcheson and Imma-
nuel Kant, did was to theorize how we might not only
laugh at others meanly and with condescension, but also
laugh at one another and ourselves kindly and while leav-
ing room for recalibration. The incongruity theory focuses
not on the blameworthy nature of blemishes and defects
(as ridicule does), but rather on their absurdity. In this
view, man is funny not because he makes mistakes, but
because he really ought to know better and avoid them.[90]

Sister Mariella's quick gloss on Catholic humor adds
to the incongruity theory both a theological dimension and

89. Gable, "Introduction to *Many-Colored Fleece*," 43.

90. John Morreall, "Philosophy of Humor," in *The Stanford En-
cyclopedia of Philosophy* (Summer 2023 Edition), ed. Edward N.
Zalta and Uri Nodelman, June 21, 2023, https://plato.stanford.
edu/archives/sum2023/entries/humor/.

a generic one. Theologically, the fact that people are made in the image of God appears to be precisely what makes human life so ripe for comedy. Indeed, critic and theologian William F. Lynch, S.J.—whose *Christ and Apollo: Dimensions of the Literary Imagination* exerted tremendous influence on O'Connor and other midcentury Catholic writers when it was published in 1960—posited that "to recall this incredible relation between mud and God is, in its own distant, adumbrating way, the function of comedy."[91]

To extend Sister Mariella's allegory, a worm cannot slip on a banana peel because a worm already belongs on the floor. But a person can slip on a banana peel and thereby render herself temporarily ridiculous, undignified, wormlike. If the person in question is wearing a crown and an ermine-trimmed robe as she tumbles to the ground, then the height from which she falls is (figuratively speaking) that much greater. And the fall of a queen from regal uprightness to wormlike supineness is presumably nothing as compared to the Fall that Adam and Eve underwent in the Garden of Eden.

We might even posit, given the enormous incongruity that results from humankind's original *telos* toward the good and our postlapsarian wandering toward lesser goods and outright evils, that humor is a further instance of *felix culpa*, of the way that God turns even our Fall into sin and death to the good of mankind. "*O felix culpa quae talem et tantum meruit habere redemptorem*," the Church

---

91. William F. Lynch, *Christ and Apollo: Dimensions of the Literary Imagination* (Belmont, NC: Wiseblood Books, 2021), 133.

recalls at Easter Vigil. "O happy fault that earned for us so great, so glorious a Redeemer." Nothing can equal the Redemption that Christ purchased for us at so high a cost. But incongruous humor can open, in its own humble way, little windows onto redemption and restoration.

Perhaps it even speaks to the manner in which divine Providence keeps our game of cultural "whisper down the lane" within safe bounds that Beattie articulated the incongruity theory of humor only forty years and a little more than a hundred miles away from David Hume's introduction of the "is-ought problem." Perhaps the potential for new confusion and more dangerous wandering occasioned by Hume's Law was offset by a gentler and more nuanced understanding of humor. If ridicule looks for a scapegoat on which to project sin and error, then incongruous humor acknowledges that human beings' sweetly absurd status as "rational sheep" is universal and offers a way back to the safety of the sheepfold.[92]

ESCHATOLOGY AND GENRE

Perhaps the most eloquent formulation of the incongruity theory of humor, and the one with the readiest applications to Christianity, can be found in Henri Bergson's essay "On Laughter" (1904). Bergson, too, presents the reader with the image of a person tripping and falling on a banana

---

92. The image of human beings as "rational sheep" comes from Byzantine monk John Geometres, *Life of the Virgin Mary*, ed. and trans. Maximos Constas and Christos Simelidis (Cambridge, MA: Harvard University Press, 2023).

peel. "The laughable element" in such a scene, he argues, "consists of a certain *mechanical inelasticity*, just where one would expect to find the wideawake adaptability and the living pliableness of a human being."[93] For him, the essence of human incongruity isn't the falling so much as the unconscious inertia that precipitated it. A fully human, fully awake person would have just stepped around the peel.

Bergson does not use the word *soul* to account for this capacity for "wideawake adaptability" and "living pliableness." But perhaps we may attribute such inexhaustible properties to a will and intellect animated by God. Bergson also does not discuss the mechanical or inert tendencies of human beings in terms of idolatry. But Psalm 115 does, suggesting that those who make idols and those "who trust in them" will become like the lesser values they mistake for absolute ones: unhearing, unseeing, mute, and motion-less.[94] When a man or woman made in the image of God

---

93. Henri Bergson, "On Laughter," in *Comedy*, ed. Wylie Sypher (Baltimore: The Johns Hopkins Press, 1980), 66–67.

94. But their idols are silver and gold,
made by human hands.
They have mouths, but cannot speak,
eyes, but cannot see.
They have ears, but cannot hear,
noses, but cannot smell.
They have hands, but cannot feel,
feet, but cannot walk,
nor can they utter a sound with their throats.
Those who make them will be like them,
and so will all who trust in them. (Psalm 115:4-8)

lapses from living icon into unseeing, unthinking idol—to reframe Psalm 115 in Bergson's terminology—"this rigidity is the comic and laughter is its corrective."[95] Laughter's corrective value, Bergson suggests, is most effective when applied in the early stages of spiritual ossification, when someone has veered into "eccentricity" or obliviousness, but not yet committed a crime, sin, or other outright harm.

Shakespeare's *King Lear*, with its odd double plot, provides an interesting case study contrasting mankind's capacity for rigidity with our capacity for change, and exploring the relation of both to genre—that is, to comedy and tragedy. In the play, not one but two foolish old men are toppled by their own scheming children. Lear begins the play as a vain, insecure, and capricious parody of a king. Gloucester, a nobleman in his court, is similarly obtuse; we first encounter him making crude jokes about the son born to him out of wedlock. Both men are especially oblivious when it comes to their children, sparking rivalry among Lear's three daughters and between Gloucester's two sons.

In the intrafamilial battles that follow, honest daughter Cordelia and legitimate son Edgar are soon banished from the kingdom. The remaining children—Regan, Goneril, and the bastard Edmund—spend the rest of the play grasping at anything they can get their hands on. First, their inheritances; then, one another. Their subplot descends into melodrama as the three wicked children dish out insults, gouge out eyes, and inflict other indignities upon their elders and themselves. At some point, their

---

95. Bergson, "On Laughter," 74.

wrongdoing begins to seem rote. They apparently can't stop looking for new wrongs to attempt, cycling through or near patricide, fratricide, plain murder, adultery, bigamy, and incest (these later offenses when Edmund proposes marriage to *both* sisters, despite the fact that Regan's husband is only newly dead and Goneril's is still alive). As the subplot flattens, the characters themselves flatten, too, into cartoonish devils. By the time Edmund is mortally wounded by his brother in a duel, surviving just long enough to receive the news that Goneril has poisoned Regan out of envy and then slain herself as a personal compliment, we are firmly in the realm of ridicule and the lowest of low comedies.

With Lear and his daughter Cordelia, however, it is a different story. When the play opens, Lear is the cartoon. His robes swamp him. He is no more capable of carrying out his duties and obligations as a king than would be a scarecrow. Lear's path to redemption winds through the grounds of toil and suffering that Adam and Eve first traversed in Genesis. Slowly, he wakes. Unevenly, he perceives and thinks and loves. By the time Lear returns fully to his senses, it is too late to reverse the disasters that his previous dereliction had set in motion. Civil war has broken out, families are torn asunder, and everything moves toward a denouement so catastrophic that for more than a century English theaters simply chucked it and replaced it with a happy ending: the innocent Cordelia is hanged; Lear's heart bursts from sorrow at her death; and his most loyal servant, Kent, dies, too, determined to follow his master even into the world to come. The height from which Lear falls at the end of the play is great, and it has much less to do with ermine-trimmed robes than with his having belatedly become pliable and fully alive.

This oddly bifurcated plot posits a clear correlation between eschatology and genre. The fate of the good characters in the play is, as Sister Mariella put it, "immeasurably serious." Their loss is felt as a tragedy. The fate of the bad characters is perhaps not a comedy as "uproariously funny" to our sensibilities as it presumably would have been for Elizabethan audiences, in an age when ridicule ruled. But, even so, an honest reader today can at least admit to feeling fairly certain that Regan, Goneril, and Edmund are all damned—and to feeling oddly unperturbed by this thought. By contrast, one wishes greatly to believe that Cordelia and Lear, if only on some other plane of reality, can still be saved.

FREE WILL AND THE LIMITS OF GENRE

Three and a half centuries after Shakespeare wrote *King Lear*, Muriel Spark would go on to cover similar ground in terms of eschatology and genre in *The Prime of Miss Jean Brodie*, though she takes an entirely different and non-deterministic approach. Published in 1961, a year after Sister Mariella's essay on satire praised Spark's earlier book *Memento Mori*, the novel pays close attention to the "*inelasticity* of character, of mind and even of body" that

Bergson identifies as "the possible sign of a slumbering activity as well as an activity with separatist tendencies, that inclines to swerve from the common centre round which society gravitates."[96]

Set in Edinburgh in the 1930s, the novel is immensely concerned with centers of gravity and with what pulls individuals toward and apart from one another. Within the larger entity that is the Marcia Blaine School, we meet a smaller group, tightly knit, of six girls clustered around one charismatic teacher, Jean Brodie. Miss Brodie prides herself, ironically, on her own elasticity of mind. By the end of the novel, however, it becomes clear that elasticity can itself become an idol, which shapes Miss Brodie first into an eccentric caricature of her former self and then into something more sinister.

In the beginning, though, Miss Brodie cuts a formidable figure. She treats the official school curriculum with disdain, instead regaling the girls with wisdom gleaned from her own reading, travels, and personal life. She takes them to tea and on walks through the city of Edinburgh. She confides in them. These extracurricular activities make the girls feel chosen, special, and they are regarded as such by the rest of the school, which nicknames them "the Brodie set." Within the set, each girl is distinguished by an epithet. Rose Stanley is "famous for sex"; Jenny Gray for beauty; Eunice Gardiner for her athletic abilities; Monica Douglas for her fiery temper and talent for mathematics; and Sandy Stranger for her vowel sounds, her Scottish

---

96. Bergson, "On Laughter," 73; emphasis in original.

accent inflected by an English mother, and for a gaze so intent she seems always to be squinting. Mary Macgregor, the sixth girl, is something of an afterthought, famous only for her utility as a scapegoat, "a silent lump, a nobody whom everybody could blame."[97]

The novel, which slips in and out of omniscient narration, carefully and gradually uncovers the flaws in this arrangement. Miss Brodie's primary criterion in selecting the girls, we learn, is actually parental neglect. Her "favourites" are "those whom she could trust; or rather those whose parents she could trust not to lodge complaints about the more advanced and seditious aspects of her educational policy."[98] In some sense, what truly bonds the set is their vulnerability in having home lives that present Miss Brodie's desire for influence with the fewest hindrances. As the girls grow and change, from ages ten to eighteen, Miss Brodie's conception of each remains static. The epithets are slowly revealed to be less a way of highlighting the unique talents of each girl and more a way of trying to determine them.

By the time that Miss Brodie attempts to engineer an extramarital affair between Rose—whose true appeal to boys her age is not sex but a vast and enthusiastic knowledge of motorcars—and the married art teacher whom Jean Brodie herself desires, Sandy has had enough. Realizing with a shock that "this was not all theory and a kind

97. Muriel Spark, *The Prime of Miss Jean Brodie* (New York: Harper Perennial, 2009), 4, 5.

98. Spark, *Prime of Miss Jean Brodie*, 25.

of Brodie game," that "Miss Brodie meant it," Sandy perceives that healthy, authoritative influence has given way to unhealthy, tyrannical intrusion. Her teacher's error is, as she sees it, a fundamentally theological one: "She thinks she is Providence, thought Sandy, she thinks she is the God of Calvin, she sees the beginning and the end."[99] Sandy subsequently provides the headmistress, long in search of a reason to fire Miss Brodie, with the concrete grounds on which to proceed. "She's a born Fascist, have you thought of that?"[100]

The novel's abhorrence of deterministic systems finds its formal counterpart in a tragicomic mode. Unlike *King Lear*, Spark's unremitting tragicomedy treats every character equally, which makes for a very, very funny read at times and a very, very dark one at others. Perhaps no character in the book is more innocent and deserving of kindness than Mary Macgregor. Clumsy, quiet, accepting of blame, and seemingly incapable of anger, Mary is treated poorly by her peers, by their teacher, and it would seem by life itself. Yet the account of her early death, aged twenty-four in a hotel fire, is absolutely pitiless:

> Back and forth along the corridors ran Mary Macgregor, through the thickening smoke. She ran one way; then, turning, the other way; and at either end the blast furnace of the fire met her. She heard no screams, for the roar of the fire drowned

99. Spark, *Prime of Miss Jean Brodie*, 38, 128, 129.
100. Spark, *Prime of Miss Jean Brodie*, 134.

the screams; she gave no scream, for the smoke was choking her. She ran into somebody on her third turn, stumbled and died. But at the beginning of the nineteen-thirties, when Mary Macgregor was ten, there she was sitting blankly among Miss Brodie's pupils. "Who has spilled ink on the floor—was it you, Mary?"

"I don't know, Miss Brodie."

"I daresay it was you. I've never come across such a clumsy girl. And if you can't take an interest in what I am saying, please try to look as if you did."

These were the days that Mary Macgregor, on looking back, found to be the happiest days of her life.[101]

Pitiless, too—at times—is the novel's treatment of Jean Brodie, who sits at the opposite end of the culpability spectrum from Mary Macgregor.

Obsessed with her own capacity for change and influence, Miss Brodie eventually finds herself in thrall to it. After her expulsion from the Marcia Blaine School, she shrinks down into a shell of her former self: self-pitying, boring, a broken record asking endlessly who betrayed her. Sandy, visiting Miss Brodie at a nursing home, is irritated by her droning whine: "It is seven years, thought Sandy, since I betrayed this tiresome woman. What does she mean by 'betray'?"[102]

---

101. Spark, *Prime of Miss Jean Brodie*, 13–14.

102. Spark, *Prime of Miss Jean Brodie*, 63.

Elsewhere, though, the novel finds a way to regard Miss Brodie, in all her human wrongness, with a gentle forbearance. Here, too, the narration is filtered through Sandy's consciousness:

> Sandy felt warmly towards Miss Brodie at these times when she saw how she was misled in her idea of Rose. It was then that Miss Brodie looked beautiful and fragile, just as dark heavy Edinburgh itself could suddenly be changed into a floating city when the light was a special pearly white and fell upon one of the gracefully fashioned streets. In the same way Miss Brodie's masterful features became clear and sweet to Sandy when viewed in the curious light of the woman's folly, and she never felt more affection for her in her later years than when she thought upon Miss Brodie silly.[103]

The tone, in this passage and the one above from the nursing home, is wily and elusive. Is Sandy's later warmth rooted in charity or in scorn? Does she have the truer view of Miss Brodie when she sees her as tiresome or as transcendent?

Sandy herself is subjected to a similar ambiguity by Spark's tragicomic mode. Her vivid interior life animates much of the novel, and yet as a character she manages simultaneously to deepen *and* flatten as the story progresses. Having apparently detected in herself too great

---

103. Spark, *Prime of Miss Jean Brodie*, 118.

a fascination with those elements of Miss Brodie's personality that she finds odious—in the end, it is Sandy and not Rose who embarks upon an affair with the art teacher, while his wife and children are away on holiday—Sandy becomes a cloistered nun, taking the name Sister Helena of the Transfiguration. As Sister Helena, she achieves renown for her "psychological treatise on the nature of moral perception, called 'The Transfiguration of the Commonplace.'"[104] Admirers flock to her cell. But—just as Jean Brodie's sin and error cannot escape being bathed in a warm, charitable light—even Sandy's religious vocation and her spiritual growth cannot escape ridicule in the novel.

As she talks to visitors through the grille in her convent cell, Sandy holds tightly to the bars. She apparently renounces the world only by the skin of her teeth; it's unclear whether her white knuckles show self-knowledge of how badly her will requires such constraints, or the lack of such knowledge. What is a lifetime's serious work for her is revealed to be merely an afternoon's diversion for others: "When she was a nun, sooner or later one and the other of the Brodie set came to visit Sandy, because it was something to do, and she had written her book of psychology, and everyone likes to visit a nun, it provides a spiritual sensation, a catharsis to go home with, especially if the nun clutches the bars of the grille."[105] One gets the sense that Sandy will win the eternal prize—with her lively mind, her

---

104. Spark, *Prime of Miss Jean Brodie*, 35.
105. Spark, *Prime of Miss Jean Brodie*, 129.

lived faith, the steady stream of readers who seek out her wisdom—and also that she is ever on the verge of losing it.

So it goes with every character in *The Prime of Miss Jean Brodie*. The other girls in the set marry, happily or unhappily. Their fates, whether deserved or undeserved, propitious or doomed, are all related with the same bemused tone—a voice always at some remove, always on the brink of amusement, ultimately impossible to pin down.

Perhaps the best sense one can make of the novel's unflinching tragicomedy is that it enacts an argument about how individual human beings will always evade representation and neat categorization (not to say predictions). The complex reality of human persons made in the image of God will resist every attempt to take its full measure, much as God himself evades our attempts to measure him. When Moses asks his name, God replies, "I AM THAT I AM" (Exod. 3:14). God cannot be contained in an epithet, because he is existence itself. And human beings are made in the image of God. This irreducible nature of existence ought to give hope to fiction writers: Despair not, for fiction—operating as it does in a realm of vicarious experience—is thus ennobled as a fitting medium through which to try to understand human persons. (Especially as against surveys, metrics, and other forms of gathering and relaying data, which—although they pose less of a challenge to the "is–ought problem"—invariably compress or short-circuit, and thus miss, the real.) Presume not, for the fiction writer must proceed with humility and a deep respect for human nature and human volition as something both irreducible and irreplaceable. No label, no epithet, no image we make of another in our minds can ever quite capture something as resplendent as a person—including, arguably, fictional persons. Even people whom we do come to know quite well are always liable to change, thanks to their capacity for free will and depending on what they hold dear, ordered or disordered as those values may be.

Sister Mariella is not wrong to remind us that each of us is heading, at every instant, toward one eternal destination or another. But *The Prime of Miss Jean Brodie* suggests that it would be impertinent to suppose we can ever know with certainty what any individual's end will be—including, perhaps, our own.

VISION AND THE METAPHYSICS
OF FICTION

Among those students who loved Sister Mariella's famed Dante course was Betty Wahl, who attended the College of St. Benedict from 1941 to 1945. Sister Mariella was quick to recognize Wahl's talent for writing and was keen on developing it. With Sister Mariella's encouragement, Wahl attended a two-month program at the University of Iowa's Writers' Workshop the summer after her junior year. During her senior year, Wahl was one of the students who snapped up an award from the *Atlantic Monthly*, an honorable mention for her essay "Dante Loves Beatrice."[106] Only a few months after Wahl graduated from St. Benedict's in June 1945 with a BA in English and a minor in French, she had already finished a draft of a novel, inspired by her time at the college.

The book's protagonist is Peggy, whom Wahl admitted was "partly myself and partly everyone I know." Her mentor, Sister Elaine, is likewise modeled after Sister Mariella, right down to the course she teaches on the *Divine Comedy*. On the first day of class, Sister Elaine tells her students that no introduction to Dante will be adequate because "the experience of Dante will always be too big to be explained." Even so, she continues, the inadequacy of paraphrase won't stop her from trying to help them

---

106. Betty Wahl, "Dante Loves Beatrice," *Atlantic Monthly* 1944–45 Atlantic Contests for College Students, 14–16.

understand: "And so, this year again, I know I shall probably draw diagrams, and use endless sentences, and you will listen very politely and not know what it is all about until you have finished the course because there are no words with which to talk about Dante except Dante's own words, and those will come later on."[107]

Sister Mariella was so enthusiastic about the novel—which was initially titled *Only the Good Are Lovely* (later, *To See the Stars*)—that she wrote to J. F. Powers, who was then working as a hospital orderly in St. Paul, Minnesota, to ask whether he might review several chapters. The manuscript reached him on October 23, 1945, and he sent his initial thoughts to Sister Mariella the same day:

> I have just finished the first chapter and without going any further would be willing to bet on the book and with more certainty on future books from Miss Wahl. The title, I think, is very bad: the first paragraph likewise. But after that it rides right along . . . . There is a very rare honesty, it seems to me, about the first chapter. I am even a little awe-struck by it.[108]

Powers agreed to come to the College of St. Benedict the second weekend in November for a chapter-by-chapter review. He arrived at St. Benedict's on November 10, 1945, and proposed to Wahl the next day. They were married on April 22, 1946.

---

107. *To See the Stars*, second version, second of two folders.

108. J. F. Powers to Mariella Gable, 23 October 1945.

The demands of family life and an unending search for the perfect home limited the amount of time and energy that Wahl could devote to her fiction. Still, she retained a sense of writerly vocation throughout her life. Well after it had become apparent that her stories could not be depended on as a reliable source of income—nor, for that matter, could his—she continued to begin each day with several hours of literary work. Wahl published three stories in *The New Yorker*, with her debut in the magazine predating Powers's by several years, and one novel, *Rafferty and Co.*, with Farrar, Straus and Giroux in 1969.

But *To See the Stars* was never published. I came across the manuscript for it in 2006, among papers generously lent to me by Katherine A. Powers—Wahl's eldest child and a formidable writer in her own right—while working on a scholarly edition of Wahl's stories for a master's thesis. At some point, Wahl labeled the box of manuscripts relating to *To See the Stars*: "Novel—original and transitional (written under the influence of Sr Mariella)." It is the sort of label that can be affixed only with distance. In an undated letter, written sometime around 1950, Wahl told her former mentor: "For my part, though I no longer believe that all the troubles of the world would be solved if everyone just read and understood Dante (and perhaps you never meant that either), it is all to the good to have once thought so."[109]

By the end of her life, Wahl further distanced herself from Sister Mariella. But she never abandoned their shared conviction that "the highest human pleasure comes from

---

109. Betty Wahl to Mariella Gable, undated, *c.* 1950.

knowing—specifically, from knowing *through vision*—something of the mystery of life," and that the vehicle most suited to conveying this kind of knowledge is fiction.[110] In a talk at the now-defunct Institute for Spirituality in Collegeville, Minnesota, in 1980, Wahl began her remarks by asking, "Where does the artist fit into the Church? I suggest we try thinking of him as a prophet." And, she continues, because "somewhere along the line man learned to think in words," the writer—who "works in words"—might be considered "the primary artist." His mission is "to see and to make others see."[111]

SIGHT AT A DISTANCE

Wahl is right. Fiction does indeed constitute a form of *tele-vision*—that is, "sight at a distance." Through fiction, an image originating in one person's mind (the writer's) is replicated or recreated in the mind of another (the reader). It is a remarkable trick, verging on magic—or miracle. But no matter how powerful an image it conveys, fiction cannot alter human nature or cure the world of all ills. Wahl ends her talk with another question, to drive home its limits:

---

110. Gable, "The Novel," 53.

111. J. F. Powers and Betty Wahl, "A Place to Stand, Yes; To Move the Earth, No" [recording of a talk at the Institute for Spirituality, St. John's University] (Collegeville, MN: St. John's University Press, 1980), transcript of cassette tape.

And now one last observation, on the effectiveness of art. Let us go back to a work in the early morning of literature. Consider the fox and the grape, the boy who cried wolf, the dog in the manger—images so effective that what Aesop saw, his visions, have passed into our language and have become part of our mental baggage. For nearly twenty-six centuries Western man has carried them about with him. How is it then that there are still dogs in the manger, cries of "wolf, wolf," and sneers at sour grapes?[112]

The impression that fiction could cure all is at least part of what Wahl seems to have renounced in her letter to Sister Mariella. But that is no reason for fiction writers to abandon their posts—certainly, Wahl herself never did—for "where there is no vision, the people perish" (Prov 29:18).

Both fiction and faith have a role to play in restoring vision to contemporary American culture. For Wahl, the fiction writer's vision must begin with "a certitude that there is somewhere else and that when time runs out, it is not the end." For "if life has no clear meaning to him, he has no reason to explain it to others."[113] For Flannery O'Connor, human vision must remain distinct from the uncomprehending, contextless mechanical vision we see all around us, for human vision alone is bolstered by depth, interpretation, charity, and a sense of the whole.

---

112. Powers and Wahl, "A Place to Stand."

113. Powers and Wahl, "A Place to Stand."

In the summer of 2016, I untangled O'Connor's ideas about human versus mechanical fiction at a writing workshop hosted by the Collegeville Institute for Ecumenical and Cultural Research. The Collegeville Institute is, as it turns out, just down the road from St. John's University, the brother institution of the College of St. Benedict, which is only a short, ten-minute drive away. (To this day, St. John's remains a men's college and St. Ben's a women's college.) As I walked around the St. John's campus, I realized that much of what I was seeing I saw as though for the second time, because I had first encountered it in Wahl's writing.

Wahl was a builder's daughter—her father, Art Wahl, built the seminary, Mary Hall, and the new monastery at St. John's University—and she was very attuned to the built environment. She never forgave famed modernist architect Marcel Breuer for taking the towers off of the old Abbey Church, and thought that if he'd had his way he wouldn't have stopped "until every last hard won red brick had tumbled down."[114] In an essay for *A Sense of Place: Saint John's of Collegeville*, she recalled falling "asleep to the sound of the cement mixer" as a child and said that "the smell of wet cement is redolent of happy memories. But concrete remains gray, drab, and heavy, the color of November, and I cannot like the Breuer church."

But that summer, every time I walked into St. John's Abbey Church, I thought of other words from Wahl—how

114. Betty Wahl, untitled essay, in *A Sense of Place: Saint John's of Collegeville*, ed. Colman J. Barry, O.S.B. and Robert L. Spaeth (Collegeville, MN: St. John's University Press, 1987), 135.

it spoke to her "of the Hoover Dam and a thousand WPA projects"—and I couldn't *help* but like the Breuer church, because it made me picture her and J. F. Powers, years ago, sitting in the balcony, wryly thinking of the aesthetics and acoustics around them as one more cross to bear.[115] At times, I half expected to see the young Betty Wahl coming around a corner in a plaid skirt and bobby socks, even as I dined with her son James and his family in a courtyard where their house in Flynntown formerly stood, even as we sat only feet away from where the bed she died in once was. If it is true that, as St. Bonaventure says, "memory is an image of eternity," then so too were these moments.[116]

After the workshop, I came home to New York, where I was then teaching at the United States Military Academy, and took down from the attic photocopies I had made of Wahl's manuscripts (the originals having been returned to Katherine Powers long before). Flipping through the drafts and fragments, I was a little stunned to see how much Sister Mariella's demeanor as a teacher—as documented in Wahl's fiction—might have shaped my own.

Because the main classroom building at West Point is built into the side of a mountain, it is largely windowless and in most rooms chalkboards cover all four walls. For the three years I taught there, although I've never been much of an artist, I found myself inventing diagram after diagram and drawing picture after picture on those wonderfully

115. Wahl, *A Sense of Place*, 135.

116. Quoted in Joshua Hren, *Contemplative Realism: A Theological-Aesthetical Manifesto* (San Francisco: Benedict XVI Institute, 2022), 40.

abundant blackboards. If the stick figures made students laugh, I rejoiced because then I knew that they were paying attention and, more than that, that they understood. The rudimentary art helped them to let their guard down, and if all went well, it gave them a picture to carry around in their minds long after class ended. Looking back, I wonder now if Sister Mariella herself wasn't holding the chalk, filling my mind with ways to make them *see*.

THE PHYSICS AND METAPHYSICS OF FICTION

One such diagram proved perennially useful on the first day of class. The German critic Wolfgang Iser defines literature as writing that is characterized by "indeterminacy"—that is, writing in which there is some kind of gap (and therefore the reader has to supply the missing logic) or an overlap of sorts (in which there are layers of meaning for the reader to discover and weigh).[117] A gap in prose is easy enough to picture: words might be missing as in Mad Libs, or redacted as in a confidential document. But multivalency in language is a bit more opaque.

To illustrate, I would draw an atom and in every class someone would have to kindly remind me exactly how many electrons go in each shell. Each electron shell could then be labeled with one layer of interpretive meaning. In Elizabeth Bishop's poem "Filling Station," for instance,

---

117. Wolfgang Iser, *The Act of Reading: A Theory of Aesthetic Response* (Baltimore: Johns Hopkins University Press, 1978).

the last line promises that "Somebody loves us all." The text does not specify explicitly who this "somebody" might be, but students have interpreted it variously as the unseen mother in the gas station, the speaker of the poem's mother or father, their own loving parents, or God. Each possible interpretation, then, is a kind of shell. Between them, meaning can jump as nimbly as electrons do, with the input of a different kind of energy from the reader. In the process of drawing this diagram—which also let the students, closer to a physics class by decades than their teacher, demonstrate their own capacity for expertise—the concept of multivalency in literature was made concrete, visible, and comprehensible.

The image of an atom leads to an unlikely and thoroughly unprovable observation. Which is that fiction, as Muriel Spark apparently intuited—along, perhaps, with all other human endeavors—does not seem to operate according to a deterministic, Newtonian universe. In the way that literature shimmers with meaning and potential, its mechanics more closely resemble the probabilistic world of quantum physics. Rules can be discerned, but nothing can be predicted with absolute certainty. A novel, or a moment in a novel, may seem incontrovertibly "Catholic" to one person and not to another. Even if transcendence could be somehow pinned down on the page, there would still be no way to predict whether it will resonate with a particular reader—or when.

Sister Mariella used the image of a bullseye to describe the kinds of subjects on which Catholic writers should train their sights. Classical and modern rhetoricians, too, have used archery as a metaphor for the act of speaking or writing effectively. Rhetorical *kairos* is, in E. C. White's definition, "a passing instant when an opening appears which must be driven through with force if success is to be achieved."[118] In other words, the artful speaker must not only aim his or her bow accurately at a target, but must also let the arrow fly at precisely the correct, opportune moment.

The rhetorical arrow launched by a novel or a poem works somewhat differently from the arrow launched by an oration. For another miraculous property of fiction is—to steal a term from Albert Einstein—its potential for "spooky action at a distance." The novelist's arrow can travel through some impossible-to-locate space for months or even decades, flying patiently across the years and across continents until a reader is ready to receive the message. This, too, seems to be an image of eternity, or perhaps of the way that a loving God is always trying to seek us out, to pierce our armor, to wait for an opportune moment when we will be ready, quickly or at last, to receive the truth.

What is that living, breathing thing that can fly for years and never lose its momentum—that waits silently in the pages of a closed book and then whirs to life again at exactly the right moment—in all the best fiction?

---

118. E. C. White, *Kaironomia: On the Will to Invent* (Ithaca: Cornell University Press, 1987).

The novelist Caroline Gordon, a Catholic convert and mentor to the young Flannery O'Connor, said it was the Holy Spirit. In 1958, Gordon presented O'Connor with a set of "first principles" for Catholic fiction writers,

> principles which I can name outright to you but which I have to approach cautiously with my secular pupils. There is only one plot. The Scheme of Redemption. All other plots, if they are any good, are splinters off this basic plot. There is only one author: The HG [Holy Ghost]. If He condescends to speak at times through a well-constructed detective story, which I think he does, he certainly will condescend to speak often through FO'C.[119]

My own experiences with textual criticism tell me that Gordon is onto something about the Holy Ghost lurking in every piece of good fiction, whether sacred or profane, because the right words in the right combination are inexhaustible in a way that points to the eternal. In the midst of collating editions of stories by Wahl and by Samuel Beckett, I have more than once marveled to find myself laughing out loud, or with tears springing to my eyes, at words that should have lost their effect on me long before.

---

119. Caroline Gordon to Flannery O'Connor, 26 January 1958, in *Good Things Out of Nazareth: The Uncollected Letters of Flannery O'Connor and Friends*, ed. Benjamin B. Alexander (New York: Convergent, 2019), 115.

No Ezra Pound expert I, but two lines from his *Cantos* stir something in my chest every time I hear them[120]:

> What thou lovest well remains,
>
> > the rest is dross.[121]

This remaining, or endurance, is important. There is something outside of us—in words and books and trees; in material reality and in the immaterial reality of other souls—waiting to be encountered.

But it is also worth noting that something *inside* of us matters, too. If the Holy Spirit lurks in the right words with a sort of potential energy, its kinetic realization comes into being only in the presence of a reader. The real measure of a movie, Walker Percy suggests in *The Moviegoer*, is not its Platonic ideal on an original film reel, but its Aristotelian instantiation at a particular place and time—when it is viewed by particular persons. "If I did not talk to the theater owner or the ticket seller" before walking into the dark theater, protagonist Binx Bolling explains, "I should be lost, cut loose metaphysically speaking. I should be seeing one copy of a film which might be shown anywhere and at any time. There is a danger of slipping clean out of space and time." Binx etches a mark with his thumbnail on

---

120. Ezra Pound, *The Cantos* (New York: New Directions, 1998), 540.

121. Pound continues:

> What thou lov'st well shall not be reft from thee
> What thou lov'st well is thy true heritage

his seat in one theater; again, the enduring is important. In another theater, he befriends the ticket seller, a grandmother of seven: "We still exchange Christmas cards. Mrs James is the only person I know in the entire state of Ohio."[122]

Likewise, the meaningful unit of a short story or a novel is not the author-corrected galley proofs, nor a signed first edition. In truth, I would argue—hopefully with Percy's blessing—that the meaningful unit of a novel or story is each time that a specific person sits down to read it, usually alone, or that a specific group of people comes together to discuss the work. One can read George Saunders's short story "Tenth of December" a dozen times, and truly one *should*, but never once will you have read it in a windowless room whose walls are covered with chalkboards, on one of which a uniformed cadet, by temperament a clown, astonished his classmates and me by drawing—in response to another cadet's asking whether "Nethers" in the story are "beaver-people"—a remarkably good beaver-person, and then, while we all struggled to take in his hitherto unknown artistic talent, erased the beaver-person as quickly and unexpectedly as he had drawn it, and left an almost audible gasp in the room. We are all a little more than we know.

There are serious examples in my mind, too. For instance, a summer school class with two students who knew well the pain of a parent facing cancer—just as in

---

122. Walker Percy, *The Moviegoer* (New York: Vintage International, 1998), 75.

"Tenth of December" Don Eber must learn to face cancer a little longer, for the sake of those whom he loves—and how the cadet whose mother was in remission crossed the room, first with words and then with footsteps, to offer encouragement and consolation to the cadet whose father was still in treatment.

In each instance: a little miracle of unexpected transcendence, a quick fall back down to earth. You would have had to be present *there* and *then* to see how it was a miniature version of almost all transcendence here below, including the transcendence we find in literature—how partial and fleeting it appears; how we are lifted up for an instant, rarely more. Even I can't go back *there* now, except in memory. But the good news is that there is always another *there* coming up, if we are open to receiving it.

And here we see how fiction requires the element of time. Narratives have a beginning, middle, and end; a joke wends its way toward a punchline. Both can offer implicit lessons in causation, quick thinking, and the value of memory. Unlike the news or most of what we read on screens today, stories and jokes both tacitly promise that it will be worth our while to *remember*, to keep track of something from start to finish, and that we will be rewarded in the end for our attention. While at West Point, I had an officemate who was charmed by the apocryphal Hemingway flash fiction—"For sale: baby shoes, never worn"—and asked his students to write six-word autobiographies. Intrigued, I sat down to write my own. What came to mind was not strictly speaking an autobiography, though perhaps it is that too, but rather an account of the silver linings given to those of us here below, who have not yet entered eternity: "Stories and laughter, our consolation prize."

SETTING OFF ON THE SEARCH

What follows from fiction's quantum unpredictability? For one thing, perhaps, we would do well to read widely and freely, as widely and freely as Sister Mariella roamed the prairies and rivers of her youth. One cannot know in advance where the Holy Spirit will turn up.

But parents and teachers should also give some thought to the fact that although Sister Mariella's childhood may have resembled the green pastures of Psalm 23, fewer and fewer children today are provided such safety and peace. An uproar over *The Catcher in the Rye* seems quaint compared to the debates looming over education today and the materials that can now be accessed instantly and sometimes accidentally by children online. So there is a case to be made for guidance and even outright censorship when it comes to the reading habits of young persons. Not the kind of censorship that discriminates and prejudges based on accidentals (especially accidentals of the author's birth or subject matter or specific four-letter words), but the kind that traditional gatekeepers once performed, which aims to ensure quality and avoid gratuitousness.

It would be imprudent to specify which kinds of books would make for a suitable training ground for early readers, though classics that have stood the test of time can provide one trustworthy starting point.

It would be even more imprudent, however, not to take into consideration at all the fact that early readers deserve special accommodation for the same reason that, say, early bowlers benefit from bumpers and early bicycle-riders benefit from training wheels. One must get one's bearings, and this does not happen instantly.

However this early formation is accomplished, so long as it is done with deliberation and care, it should be only a temporary constraint. Sister Mariella was adamant that readers did not need to be coddled, and that to do so would be both patronizing and dangerous, given the realities of the world in which we live. "Edification at the expense of truth is a terribly doubtful good," she wrote to Bishop Busch in 1943. Twenty years later, in a letter to Father Egan, she repeated the sentiment: "Protection is no part of education."[123]

Instead, she would have us trust that negative fiction—so long as it is not crap—can reveal "suffering's ability to toss the soul toward God," and that fiction which perceptively diagnoses modern ills without offering clear solutions can be enough to set readers off on what Walker Percy calls "the search." By this, Percy means the search

---

123. Mariella Gable to Joseph Busch, 12 May 1943, quoted in Hynes, Introduction, xxiv. Mariella Gable to Thomas Egan, 16 December 1963, quoted in Hynes, Introduction, xxxv.

for meaning, for humankind's place in the cosmos, both as a species and each man and woman as an individual. Gilson might say that this search, though it rarely consciously presents itself as such, is at bottom a search for the understanding, fear, and love of God that will bring to our restless hearts peace at last and lasting peace.

We must trust, too, that—as a friend I met at the Collegeville Institute, Laura Kelly Fanucci, once said—"You can't miss your *kairos*." But nor can anyone else find it for you.

My own reading life testifies to the potential for correction—for straightening out—that comes from wandering freely through reams of pages. From kindergarten through a doctorate, I attended exclusively secular institutions, first public K–12 schools and then private colleges. All the while, I read for pleasure and discovery, which, according to Maria Tatar, an expert on fairy tales, is exactly what draws children to stories in the first place: the worst-case scenarios they present along with, usually, a way out. I read in this fashion well into the twenty-second grade, never fully aware of why fiction had such a hold on me. In retrospect, there are hints that I was searching for something in books that I couldn't name, and which I now think is what Sister Mariella called the eschatological dimension of fiction. I felt impatient with novels that only scratched the surface of human experience. When my committee asked, after the second oral exam in my PhD program—which involved sounding out inchoate ideas for a dissertation—if I wanted to edit the fiction of John

Updike, whose papers had then recently been acquired by Harvard University, the question (to quote Sister Mariella) filled me with rage. I was looking for authors who had depth, wisdom, vision, and truth, and I was frustrated that I hadn't been able to communicate that.

A decade later I find that as a teacher, paradoxically, I don't particularly want to communicate the vision I eventually found to my students. I want primarily to assign them books that are a joy to read; as well as books that contain images both vivid and true, images that will stay with them and resurface as needed down the line in moments of overwhelming grief or terror or love; and above all books whose moments of indeterminacy I genuinely need their help to untangle and understand. In my mind's eye, I sometimes see the trajectory of my reading life—from *The Baby-sitters Club* series to J. D. Salinger's *Nine Stories* to Thomas Pynchon's *V.* to Søren Kierkegaard's *Sickness unto Death* and everything in between—as something like Robert Smithson's earthwork *Spiral Jetty*, which I must have encountered somewhere in a lecture on site-specific art. A jagged swirl, moving piecemeal and labyrinth-like, toward the center of something. I would not preempt anyone's journey from wandering into truth by telling them too much about mine.

CONCLUSION

THE LIMITS OF INFLUENCE AND THE IMPORTANCE OF FORM

Powers's early enthusiasm for Wahl's fiction did not stand the test of time. For most of their marriage, the two did not share works in progress with one another. When they did, his comments on her manuscripts could be brutal. Powers's job in the marriage was to be the artist, full-stop. His work came first, often well before pressing familial and financial concerns, as is unflinchingly documented in *Suitable Accommodations*, a selection of Powers's correspondence carefully woven by their eldest daughter, Katherine A. Powers, into the unwritten novel of family life that her father always wanted to write, but didn't. Money was often in short supply in the Powers household. As the couple welcomed five children, albeit somewhat grudgingly, and undertook a series of moves—usually back and forth between Ireland, where the cost of living was lower and the culture more suited to their tastes, and the American Midwest—time was in short supply, too. All practical, day-to-day matters such as cooking, child-rearing, house-hunting, and keeping everyone fed and in clean and mended clothes were left entirely in Wahl's capable hands.

Somehow she still carved out time each morning to devote to her own writing. But her letters tell a story largely of sacrifice. Wahl believed so thoroughly in her husband's calling and talent that she was willing to endure genteel poverty, long stretches living effectively as a single parent, and much else on its behalf. She found much to be desired in their endless search for the right home; in the order that had to be established anew after each move; and in the demands of parenting five small children. Two days after the birth of her youngest child, Jane, in Ireland, Wahl wrote in her journal, "Five, five, five. How did it come about? I keep repeating Fr. Egan—they are, in the end, the only thing that will have mattered. I believe it, I feel it. And yet they defy peace and order and what of art—of Jim's if not mine."[124] She expected her husband's stories to be read for a century or several, that they should last about as long as a tree. It took more effort to trust that her children's souls would last for all eternity.

In 1975, Wahl and Powers returned to Minnesota for good. There, St. John's University provided them with faculty housing and offered Powers a teaching position in the English department. The last years of Wahl's life were marked by recurring battles with breast cancer, which metastasized. She died from the disease on May 12, 1988, at the age of sixty-four.

On the morning of the day she died, Powers brought Wahl a small piece of paper with a menu written on it and boxes to check for her preferred breakfast items. She checked two boxes: one for eggs, which she ate but could not keep down, and the other for a kiss. On her deathbed,

---

124. Betty Wahl, journal, 4 July 1958. The journal is housed with Katherine A. Powers's collection of her parents' papers.

as Katherine Powers recalled years later, "Betty cursed the nuns at St. Ben's. She said she had been sold a bill of goods."[125] Perhaps Sister Mariella most of all, Wahl felt, had promoted the virtues of the writing life and the family life without truly understanding either, nor how the two might be in conflict.

Less than four years later the couple's second eldest child died from breast cancer. Mary Farl Powers was then forty-three years old and a celebrated visual artist in Ireland at the height of her career, known for her print-making, etching, and lithography. The cancer was fatal only because she had so wished to avoid the same fate as her mother that she never went to the doctor at all. She died at home of untreated breast cancer, in great pain, an end almost unheard of in the Western world in the late twentieth century. After her death, her former partner, the poet Paul Muldoon, wrote the long poem "Incantata" about her. In it is refracted his memory of Mary Farl Powers and her family, the vision he has in a dream of

> your mother, Betty Wahl,
> who took your failing, ink-stained hand
> in her failing, ink-stained hand,
> and together you ground down that stone by sheer
> force of will.[126]

---

125. Katherine A. Powers to Cassandra Nelson, 6 July 2007, email.

126. Paul Muldoon, "Incantata," in *The Annals of Chile* (New York: Farrar, Straus and Giroux, 1994), 16.

In Muldoon's telling, Mary's Catholic upbringing had impressed upon her something closer to the coldness of deism or the cruelty of Calvinist predestination: "The fact that you were determined to cut yourself off in your prime / because it was pre-determined has my eyes abrim."

Lines of influence, it would seem, are not like other lines. They do not cover the shortest distance between two points; they are not straightforward. They do not always go where we expect them to go.

The effect that our words and actions will have on another is impossible to predict in advance; perhaps even impossible to know definitively in retrospect. When it comes to culture, we human persons—with our perennial tendency to ego and to error—are always inserting ourselves into the game of "telephone." Acting as unconsciously as the man who slips on a banana peel in Bergson's essay, we assign too much emphasis to one thing and not enough to another. We assume that what resonates with us will resonate instantly and automatically with our listener, too. We wrongly think a story is more about us than it really is—or less. The classic personality, as Sister Mariella points out, is never fully achieved. Consequently, we are all always a little warped, and we pass on messages accordingly.

The saving grace in this equation is form. There is an order to every work of art, a set of governing principles which unites it and makes it function as an organic whole. When the substrate of meaning that animates a particular work of art overlaps with God's governing principles—that is, with the order and design we find in God's created world and in normative morality—then the artist has succeeded in the most meaningful way possible.

It would seem that intention is not necessary for an artist to achieve success at this level. Nor are consciously held beliefs about God or metaphysics—whether they are sound, unsound, or nonexistent. Dedication to craft alone appears to be the price of entry to potential transcendence. John Updike wrote an unimpressive novel about faith called *In the Valley of the Lilies*, but he also wrote a quietly beautiful account of Our Lady of Guadalupe's appearances to St. Juan Diego in "The Miracle of Tepeyac" (included in Sister Mariella's anthology *Many-Colored Fleece*).

The best fiction writers—those beloved by readers and critics, both secular and religious, for generations—often seem to sense that they are insufficient to the demands of their vocation. They speak of how works of art arrive whole, unbidden. They mistrust their own talents and are haunted by the possibility, even after a great success, that they may never succeed again. Muldoon discerns this tendency to self-doubt in Mary Farl Powers. She possesses "what seems always true of the truly great," he writes: "a winningly inaccurate / sense of your own worth," a readiness to "second-guess / yourself too readily by far."

Perhaps such doubt is a form of humility and preparation for grace. The word "inspiration" comes from the Latin *inspirare*, meaning to breathe or blow into. God instructs Ezekiel to say to the dry bones, "I will cause breath to enter you, and you shall live. I will lay sinews on you, and will cause flesh to come upon you, and cover you with skin, and put breath in you, and you shall live; and you shall know that I am the LORD" (Ezek. 37:5-6).

The bards of antiquity spoke of muses. Perhaps we may speak of the Holy Spirit as the source behind those shimmering moments of indeterminacy in literature. At Pentecost, the Holy Spirit descended upon the disciples and gave to each the gift of speech in another language. Just so do literary texts speak to us as individuals, with meaning that reveals itself one intellect and one instant at a time, delivering precisely the message each reader needs at precisely the moment he or she is ready to receive it.

Perhaps the flickers of meaning and transcendence we find in literature are designed to guide us, patiently and at our own pace, toward an encounter with Christ, the Incarnate Word, in whom content and form are perfectly united and through whom all things were made.

A short story by David Foster Wallace is the closest thing I have yet found to Sister Mariella's vision for contemporary fiction. It gives insight into what she called the psychology of goodness and into the kind of heroism needed for family life today. Wallace's papers, which are housed at the Harry Ransom Center in Austin, Texas, show that he thought deeply about metaphysics, though not always soundly. He tried twice to join the Catholic Church, but by his own account "flunked" the Rite of Christian Initiation for Adults both times. At other moments, he pursued Buddhism and other Eastern religions. Wallace struggled with deep depression for most of his adult life, and the scattershot references to irreconcilable faith traditions in the notes and manuscripts for his last novel, *The Pale King*, give the impression of a drowning man reaching out for whatever might keep his head above water. "Good People" emerged from those manuscripts. It was first published as a stand-alone story in *The New Yorker* in 2007 and, after Wallace died by suicide the following year, was also woven into a posthumously edited version of *The Pale King* in 2011.

The story contains almost no external action, just a couple sitting at a picnic table in a park. They're young and unmarried, college students, serious Christians; and she is expecting a child. They've decided on an abortion, but on the day of the appointment Sheri Fisher has realized she cannot go through with it. There isn't a word of direct dialogue in the story. Everything that passes between them is mediated through the consciousness of Lane Dean, Sheri's boyfriend, and I know of nothing else in contemporary fiction that makes such an explicit attempt to show a will and an intellect thrashing about in search of godliness:

> He so fervently wished it never happened. He felt like he knew now why it was a true sin and not just a leftover rule from past society. He felt like he had been brought low by it and humbled and now did understand and believe that the rules were there for

a reason. That the rules were concerned with him personally, as an individual. He'd promised God he had learned his lesson. But what if that, too, was a hollow promise, from a hypocrite who repented only after, who promised submission but really only wanted a reprieve? He might not even know his own heart or be able to read and know himself. He kept thinking also of 1 Timothy 6 and the hypocrite therein who *disputeth over words*. He felt a terrible inner resistance but could not feel what it was it so resisted. This was the truth.[127]

As he sits at the picnic table, Lane feels himself "frozen" and hovering at the edge of hell. The word he has not let himself say aloud or even think is "love." A vision of damnation comes to him in the form of "two great and terrible armies within himself, opposed and facing each other, silent." Whether they battle or stay motionless, he fears becoming "two hearted, a hypocrite to yourself either way."[128] The will he is searching for is outside of himself.

Looking around the park, at a lake, Lane experiences a quiet revelation: "He was given then to know that through all this frozen silence he'd despised he had, in truth, been praying all the while, or some little part of his heart he could not know or hear had, for he was answered now with a type of vision, what he later would call within his own

---

127. David Foster Wallace, *The Pale King* (New York: Back Bay Books, 2012), 42.

128. Wallace, *The Pale King*, 43.

mind a vision or *moment of grace*."[129] In this vision, Lane is absolved. He is "not a hypocrite, just broken and split off like all men."[130] For a moment he sees himself and Sheri "as Jesus might see them—as blind but groping, wanting to please God despite their inborn fallen nature."[131] When Sheri releases all claim on him, wishes him the best, and says that she will raise the baby alone, Lane sees through her steady voice and calm demeanor. He "has been given to know her heart," and to know that her words are a "terrible make-or-break gamble born out of the desperation in Sheri's soul, the knowledge that she can neither do this thing today nor carry a child alone and shame her family."[132] In this moment of spiritual insight—which is "given" to him—something inside of Lane shifts its focus from self to other, from sureness to curiosity, from fear to love. The story ends with a series of questions, culminating with: "What if he is just afraid, if the truth is no more than this, and if what to pray for is not even love but simple courage, to meet both her eyes as she says it and trust his heart?"[133]

When I last taught this story, I saw firsthand Sister Mariella's claim that the "chaos, bitterness, and despair" of contemporary life has left people—or at least the young people who ended up in my classes at West Point—with a sizable need and appetite for "great fiction of spiritual

129. Wallace, *The Pale King*, 43–44.

130. Wallace, *The Pale King*, 44.

131. Wallace, *The Pale King*, 44.

132. Wallace, *The Pale King*, 44.

133. Wallace, *The Pale King*, 45.

affirmation."[134] I never once heard a conservative student protest the story's reference to abortion, nor a liberal student complain about the citations of Scripture. They liked seeing a conscience wrestle with itself on the page; they knew the struggle well. One prior-service cadet, whose glower was authoritative enough to hinder class discussion for the first part of the semester and who only slowly took an interest in the course, proclaimed "Good People" the best thing he had ever read.

Later on in *The Pale King*, we see a framed photo of Sheri and the baby on Lane's desk. His white-collar office job is soul-crushing, and the highlight of each workday is glancing over to see the smiling faces of his wife and son.

What does it mean that I can see Lane Dean's desk in my mind's eye? Only one corner of it is in focus, with a calendar and a picture frame and, sometimes, a half-filled coffee mug. The image flickers and then goes out. But it's there, and it has been there for ten years. In a different work, an essay on cruise ships, Wallace wrote that "even a really beautiful, ingenious, powerful ad (of which there are a lot) can never be any kind of real art" because "an ad has no status as a gift."[135] An advertisement clearly seeks to *get* something from the reader, namely money. But what is it that art seeks to *give*? For Sister Mariella, the answer is salvation. She looked forward to a heaven like Dante's

134. Gable, "Introduction to *Many-Colored Fleece*," 30.

135. David Foster Wallace, "A Supposedly Fun Thing I'll Never Do Again," in *A Supposedly Fun Thing I'll Never Do Again: Essays and Arguments* (New York: Little, Brown and Co., 1997), 289.

Paradiso: "the scattered leaves of all the universe—at last all together in a single volume, love the binding."[136] And in the best Catholic fiction, she saw this heaven come down to earth, glimpses of what it means to see and know and love truly, a trail of breadcrumbs to point the soul home.

---

136. Gable, "Personality and Catholic Fiction," 20.

ACKNOWLEDGMENTS

I am grateful to the Powers family for their kindness and generosity—most especially to Katherine A. Powers for almost two decades of friendship, and also for the warmth and hospitality I have received from Jane and Jonathan in Ireland; Boz, Bridget, James, and Emily in Minnesota; and Hugh, Tom, and Bob Groves in Massachusetts. I am also thankful to the Powers Family Literary Property Trust for permission to quote from correspondence and manuscripts relating to Betty Wahl and J. F. Powers.

At the College of St. Benedict, I am grateful to archivist Peggy Roske and the late Sister Nancy Hynes, O.S.B., who generously shared her in-progress scholarship with me years ago and whose edited collection of Sister Mariella Gable's essays made this book possible. My warm thanks are also due to Al, Carly, and Alison Watts, who kindly hosted me during my first pilgrimage to St. Ben's.

A number of people have encouraged me over the years to write about faith and fiction, including Christopher Ricks at Boston University; the late Barbara Kiefer Lewalski, Louis Menand, John Stauffer, James Wood, Laura Forsberg, Michelle De Groot, and Stephen Tardif at Harvard University; R. R. Reno, Matthew Schmitz, and Julia Yost at *First Things*; Thomas Baker, Paul Baumann, Griffin Oleynick, and Dominic Preziosi at *Commonweal*; Veery Huleatt and Dori Moody at *Plough*; Alison Arant, Eric Bennett, Robert Donahoo, Bruce

Gentry, and Christina Bieber Lake at the 2014 NEH Summer Institute on Flannery O'Connor; Christopher Check of Catholic Answers; Fr. Paul N. Check of the Shrine of Our Lady of Guadalupe in La Crosse, Wisconsin; Dorothy Bass, Carla Durand, Laura Kelly Fanucci, Stina Kielsmeier-Cook, Michael N. McGregor, Don Ottenhoff, Mark R. Schwehn, and others whom I met through the Collegeville Institute for Ecumenical and Cultural Research; Robert F. Cochran, Jr., Matthew Crawford, Emma Bedor Hiland, Mark Hoipkemier, James Davison Hunter, Andrew Lynn, and Paul Nedelisky at the Institute for Advanced Studies in Culture; and Anthony Domestico, David Mahan, and Tanya Walker of the Christian Poetics Initiative. I am grateful to all of them.

In addition, I am especially indebted to Randy Boyagoda, Joshua Hren, and John Wilson for their encouragement about this project specifically; to William Ghosh for helping bring both the story and the structure of this book into focus; to Tony Bolos, Daniel G. Hummel, Susan Swanke, and others at the Lumen Center for the Study of Christianity and Culture for their assistance in figuring out the conclusion; and to those readers who wrote or emailed to tell me that the essay version of this book resonated with them. At Wiseblood Books, Joshua and Brittney Hren deserve immense thanks for their patience and friendship, Janille Stephens for her thoughtful copyedits, John Gray for his diligent proofreading, and Mary Finnegan for carefully and promptly shepherding the manuscript into a finished book.

Not only am I grateful *to* the people above, I am grateful *for* them, and above all for my daughter Evelyn Josephine and the wonderful community we found at St. Mary, Mother of God, Parish in Menomonee Falls, Wisconsin, who kept us afloat while this book was being completed.

Though Christopher Ricks does not share my faith, he has nevertheless taught me a good deal about it, not least that careful attention to carefully chosen words is good preparation for a life of grace. "Gratitude is among those human accomplishments that literature lives to realize," he writes in "The Best Words in the Best Order," an essay collected in *Along Heroic Lines*. "Art enjoys the power not only to voice gratitude but to prompt it, even to restore us to a state in which *grateful* might come again to mean at once *feeling gratitude* and *feeling pleasure*—as though it once was, and ought always to be, impossible to be granted something gratifying and not be grateful for it." May it be so, newly or again, for us all.

ABOUT THE AUTHOR

Cassandra Nelson is a visiting fellow at the Lumen Center in Madison, Wisconsin, and an associate fellow at the University of Virginia's Institute for Advanced Studies in Culture. Before that, she taught literature and composition at the United States Military Academy. She received her BA in English and MA in Editorial Studies from Boston University and a PhD in English literature from Harvard University. Her edition of Samuel Beckett's *More Pricks than Kicks* was published by Faber and Faber in 2010.

WISEBLOOD ESSAYS IN
CONTEMPORARY CULTURE

Wiseblood Essays in Contemporary Culture offer in-depth interpretations of literature and art at large from a distinctly Catholic vantage point, while also championing and criticizing notable Catholic contributions to culture.

SELECTED TITLES

Jane Austen's Darkness
Julia Yost

Christopher Beha: Novelist in a Postsecular World
Katy Carl

T.S. Eliot: Culture and Anarchy
James Matthew Wilson

Christianity and Poetry
Dana Gioia

Poetry and Mysticism
Raïssa Maritain

Death Comes for the Cathedrals
Marcel Proust

A shorter version of this essay originally appeared in *First Things*.